A Pilgrim's Journey into the Divine Will
"Heaven Speaks to All People and All Nations."

By Stacy Mal

Independently Published
ISBN: 9781549551024

Cover Design by Stacy Mal
Cover photos purchased from Canstock Photo.

All messages from Heaven referenced in this book have been taken
from the Holy Love Ministries website (www.HolyLove.org) unless
otherwise noted.

To my children.
May your path always be laden with grace. And may you always be close to your "other Momma."

A FIRST HAND WITNESS

When a soul has been touched by the incomprehensible grace of the Divine Will of God, so well described by Stacy Mal in the pages of this book, there is little to add. Her story of spiritual transformation related in these pages says all that is necessary.

What is worthy of commentary concerning Stacy's spiritual turnaround, however, is the ultimate source from which it came. After reading a book about apparitions of the Blessed Virgin Mary taking place in a little village in the mountains of Bosnia-Hercegovina, a place named Medjugorje, Stacy felt the first pangs of conversion; or, as she put it, "re-conversion" of a fallen-away Catholic.

A little later, Stacy discovered through a friend another alleged apparition site, but this one in the state of Ohio, a little closer to home. Holy Love Ministries in Elyria, a suburb of Cleveland, would soon become like a second home for Stacy.

The result of many visits to and discoveries at Holy Love Ministries has led to this mesmerizing and totally open first-hand witness by Stacy of the grace pouring out of this holy place. Thousands of people from throughout North America and Central America have journeyed there. Like Stacy, they have found the Divine Will of God and a transformed life.

The first-hand witness of a soul saved by the holy grace of God's love, which is really what the Divine Will of God is, is powerful spiritual medicine. But discerning such claimed miraculous events of apparitions of heavenly souls takes Church-grounded theology and blind faith acceptance.

It is not a choice between the two. One cannot stand without the other.

To "prove" the authenticity of the claimed supernatural ongoing events at Holy Love Ministries, theology is required to confirm the content, structure and message of the apparitions through adherence to Church doctrine and Holy Scripture. To date, no message or event through the apparitions has fallen outside of these guidelines. Blind faith witness as given here by Stacy, produces the good fruits that are borne out by a dramatic change in daily life, and an enthusiastic, voluntary conformance to its central message over a period of time.

The ongoing spiritual conversion of Stacy Mal formed and honed at Holy Love Ministries, and told in the pages of this book, is good fruit. I feel her first-hand witness will lead to a plentiful crop of other souls that will give off a hundred-fold.

~Wayne Weible

TABLE OF CONTENTS

INTRODUCTION

"Seek the straight path, My children. Seek the simple path of Holy Love. It is not new. My Son offered it to you when He was amongst you. I come only to help humanity rediscover the truth. I will bless you."
~Blessed Mother (October 20, 1998)

"...do not be surprised that many disbelieve. It is a difficult path I call you upon—one not easily traveled."
~Jesus (March 31, 1999)

"Oh, that souls would find this path! Oh, that they would travel it!"
~Jesus, (September 16, 1998)

"Always, always, I am with you. Make this journey into Divine Love. I am traveling with you."
~Jesus (January 3, 1999)

"You must pray for impoverished souls. They travel the road to perdition and do not realize it...But you have the key. You know the path. Now you must make it known."
~Blessed Mother (July 27, 1996)

INTRODUCTION

If someone would have told me in my younger days (when I had washed my hands of religion) that someday I would write a book on apparitions of the Virgin Mary, I probably would have told them they were out of their mind.

At that time, I was your typical fallen-away Catholic—turned off by liturgy, uninformed to decree, estranged from the Word. The Virgin Mary was the farthest thing from my mind at the time. But, after taking many wrong roads, I came back to the Church by the grace of God. A few years later, I happened upon an apparition site in Ohio.

There, I realized I was spiritually standing at the beginning of a lifelong marathon. A marathon that was destined to someday end at the threshold of eternity. The missionaries at the site gave me a map to salvation, which they called it the United Hearts revelation. They gave me a bottle of spring water, and pointed to a statue of the Blessed Mother.

"You begin over there," they said.

I didn't understand what they meant, but I walked in Her direction. When I got to Her, it was as if She unveiled a small path that She had been protecting... a path that showed faint evidence of footprints. I took a deep breath—and just like that, my journey of faith began.

It wasn't always so simple, however. The path

(though straightforward) is a difficult one. At points it seems lonesome, other points scary. There have been many times I have wanted quit, times the path seemed so dark I could scarcely take a step forward, times I was so cold with apathy and lack of prayer I thought my soul might shrivel up on the spot.

But, each time, I found the Blessed Mother was with me. Each time, She wrapped me in Her mantle, shone Her light on the path, and I saw the Lord waiting for me in the distance. He took my hand and called me by name.

"Stacy..." He sighed, joyfully.

Unable to look ahead, I closed my eyes. "You lead," I told Him. I surrendered my will (that convoluted, internal compass of mine) and He smiled. We walked so closely together that He took over my being. It was no longer I who walked the path, but He who drove my body onward. And each step we took together unveiled more and more of the real me, the creature God created me to be. I found new dimensions of my soul—hidden potential, fortitude, purpose, and love.

That is not to say, however, that I was never ever again startled by a noise coming from the fog, or enticed by the calling of my name from the outer darkness. That is not to say I never again sought my internal compass or let go of His hand—Because I did. I let go of His hand several times, running off course, leaving my trusty map lying in a mud puddle.

In fact, there were several times I got so off track I wound up all the way back at the starting line—and this could easily happen again in the future, as I am one of the weaker creatures walking this road to salvation.

But, that's the beauty of the journey. Our Lady is always there, waiting for me to call on Her for help. And the instant I do, She wraps me in Her mantle again, and takes me to Jesus—who smiles and takes my hand again.

I say all this to you so that you understand this book is but a mere testimony to a pathway that I—a fallen-away, then reconverted Catholic—never knew existed before. I use my journey as an example because it is the only way I know how to tell this story. I can only explain it the way that it happened to me (over many, long years).

Though it should be clear: this is not *my* story; it's *Heaven's* story—a story about a path to salvation that the Father created for souls; a path on which the Son stands waiting to walk with us. It is a path on which the Spirit blows in order to enflame the flickering little souls in danger of being puffed out by the enemy.

This is a story about a path that the Blessed Mother not only protects, but has described in great detail to a visionary named Maureen, living just outside of Cleveland,

Ohio—a visionary who has been charged with the chief task of distributing the map and encouraging wandering souls. She is a visionary who unfortunately has come face-to-face with those whose goal it is to thwart Heaven's plans, to condemn and close up this trail to paradise.

This is a story chosen specifically for these times (the end times), when in a last, desperate attempt to snatch souls from God, Satan has carved out his own grandiose pathways—pathways that are enticing and pleasurable to travel, but prove to be nothing more than dead end roads.

This story has been chosen for these times because we have deserted the one, true path (albeit unintentionally). We have allowed it to become so overgrown that we might never find it again without the map Our Lady gave to Maureen.

So, if you are reading this, please understand the grave responsibility you now have by hearing this message. Our Lord stands lonesome and eager on a path in the wilderness, waiting for hearts to consume and enflame. He waits and He waits...trapped in the brambles that grow on neglect and misused free will. Understand, friends, this pathway will not clear itself. It is only through the foot traffic of many souls that the passage of the New Covenant will ever be as the Father intended it.

So, now, I beg you. Remove your boots, weighted by

doubt and skepticism, and put on your walking shoes. Open your hearts to this testimony—to the Love and Mercy that pave the way. For I can tell you: you will find no other passageway on earth as consuming and life-giving as this one. I don't deserve to know this. I can't explain it theologically. But I know for certain that I must testify to it...because Heaven desires to transform an innumerable number of other souls along this path as well.

I also know there will be some who will not accept this testimony. Some I realize are content on other, worldly paths. They are set too firmly in their way and will not consider an alternate route. They will, therefore, criticize and scrutinize the map Maureen has shown to me. They may even spit at it and try to destroy it. But that is okay. Such has been the case with every other story surrounding a true apparition. The devil hates that which brings about his demise. In time, all will know the Truth. And in the meantime, I know the Lord will sustain me, just as He has in the past.

So without further delay, I would like to tell you a story....

CHAPTER 1

"The Invitation"

"I desire that they know My presence is always and continually here. Many and profound graces are yet to come."
~Blessed Mother (June 24, 1998)

I extend My invitation to all nations to come to this site and partake of the message of Holy Love. This message is all-embracing, all-encompassing. The prodigies of grace extended here are proof and the fruits of My coming to you. I desire processions come in prayer to the Spring Heaven has given."
~Blessed Mother (April 20, 1996)

"My dear children...thank you for accepting My invitation to share this moment in time with Me. I have come to offer you the embrace of My Heart...Please accept My invitation to apostleship, and spread My message."
~Blessed Mother (January 24,
1998)

"I am about to ask My Son to multiply the loaves and fishes— these being the graces at My prayer site. Those who accept My invitation will find there is no end to My generosity. When you joined me at another of My apparition sites far away, you found it difficult to return—difficult to tear yourself away. Such will it be here, for those who respond to Me."
~Blessed Mother (February 20, 1998)

I sat in my office, late one winter night, with only a small desk lamp lighting the room. The sound of my rickety space heater nearly lulled me to sleep. I rubbed my eyes and yawned.

"Think," I told myself. "What should we cover in the spring issue?" I waited...and waited. "Something unique for Easter..." I muttered.

But nothing came to me. I leaned my head back on my tall chair and put my feet on the desk. I watched the Windows logo dance around my computer monitor. But still, nothing came to me.

I was seconds away from closing up shop, when something caught my eye. A black leather strap was sticking out from behind the filing cabinet. I leaned down and pulled out an old, travel briefcase that I had used at a previous job, years ago.

Talk about a blast form the past! I pulled out old post-it notes, an overly scheduled calendar, coupons, chewed pens...and something else. It was a book, called *Medjugorje: The Message* written by Wayne Weible. From the description on the back, it seemed to be a book about the apparitions of the Virgin Mary in Medjugorje, Bosnia. I hadn't read the book, and I had no idea where the book came from, I assumed I had bought it on a business trip, though, while stuck in some airport. That was typical in those days.

I began to leaf through it. Suddenly, I had the strangest sensation. Everything around me seemed to dissipate and I felt inside myself that I should write about Marian apparitions in the next issue. It would be the Easter issue, but because this was a bimonthly magazine, it would also cover the month of May, when Catholics typically honor the Blessed Mother.

"But, wait a minute." I thought. "This magazine is nondenominational. Marian apparitions are a Catholic thing. I can't do that."

Staring at the back of the book I noticed the author, Wayne Weible, was a *Protestant* journalist at the time he wrote this book. It was as though the book had spoken to my heart and said, "Yes, you *can* write about this—Wayne did."

"Okay," I thought. "So he was a Protestant. But still...I can't spend the Easter issue on Mary. The non-Catholics will have a field day with it. Besides, what will the advertisers think?"

The idea seemed ridiculous, but it was like the book was speaking to me on a very interior level, and wouldn't let up, dispelling every objection I had to writing the article. Before long, I had solidly made up my mind.

I couldn't explain my reasons verbally, but I felt in my soul that I had to do it. And so, for whatever reason, I put it on the schedule. It was official. We were going to feature Marian apparitions in the Easter issue of *The Gist* magazine.

While preparing the issue, though, I encountered a great deal of resistance. Word got out that I was working on an apparitions piece, and it had raised some eyebrows. Inwardly, while writing the article, I met some resistance as well.

I knew in my soul that this was important. But I wondered if featuring a historically Catholic phenomenon in a nondenominational publication, during the Easter season, would be well-received or journalistically suicidal. I even wondered if my colleagues would have any kind of respect for me as Editor-in-Chief of this magazine, after it was all said and done.

What's more, a woman who I had never met before, came to see me about the issue. Her name was Candy Kelly, and she brought me information on apparitions taking place in Elyria, OH, just outside of Cleveland. She brought pictures, booklets, messages. While I had heard of this place before, I wasn't quite sure what to do with it. I mean, from what I knew, the Church hadn't given it the seal of approval yet— and honestly, it seemed a little far-fetched to me.

Still, there was something about this woman. She was not eccentric. She was not pushy. She was just a simple, Christian mom with grown children. She sat there, telling me of her experience. And I had to admit, the pictures she brought with her *were* amazing. I could see that she believed with her whole soul, and it was semi-contagious.

"But come on," I thought, "The Blessed Mother in Cleveland?"

I continued writing the article, tip-toeing around solely Catholic beliefs, unsure how or even *if* I should include the Ohio apparitions. My fears materialized on paper. The article was a big, unorganized mess... a disconnected series of inconsequential paragraphs. Truly, this apparitions piece was turning out to be a disaster.

During this same time, my social life encountered its own share of resistance—business associates, friends, and relatives who expressed their Christian objections openly and with such fervor. That week, it seemed every which way I turned resistance was hitting me in the face. And it hurt, deep in my soul.

I felt alone in my convictions. I felt out-powered by the opposition and scared—not only for my faith, but for the magazine which was trying to re-kindle Christianity in our community. I also felt sad. I wondered: if the opposition has upset *me* this much, what must it be doing to Jesus?

Personally, and professionally, it began to take its toll on me. I developed a bad case of writer's block. My mind was spinning—even in my dreams, I felt the effects.

One night, I dreamt I was sitting in my living room, and my mother walked in my front door. It was odd because my mother was living in Virginia at the time. Also, she grabbed my mail from the mailbox. "You got a post card from Heaven," she said. She was holding up a card with a very dynamic rainbow on it. The post card read, "You're invited! You have been called."

In the dream, my mom stared at me inquisitively. "So, are you going to do it?" she asked. For some reason, her question really (and I mean *really*) affected me.

"I don't know... I just don't know." I told her.

Then, I woke up.

The dream might *seem* simple enough, but the emotions I felt in that dream still lingered after I woke up— and the dream itself was so clear. In fact, I could see the post card in my mind perfectly when I awoke... as if I were still looking at it in the present moment.

I couldn't shake the strong feelings I had afterwards either. It was almost as if it had *really* happened. And I felt as though my mother was still waiting for my answer. So, I called my mom that morning and told her about it. I told my husband, Tim, also. I told them about the clarity of the dream and the deep emotions that it triggered. They appeased me, but with an understandable hint of confusion.

"Huh..." They said, awkwardly. "Yeah, you're right. That *is* weird."

Hearing myself describe the dream out loud made me wonder about my sanity. Why was I getting all worked up over a dream about a rainbow, on a postcard?

"I need a vacation." I thought.

With that, I decided to take a day trip over to Elyria, OH and visit Maranatha Spring and Shrine, the home of Holy Love Ministries—where apparently Mary has been appearing. After all, if something *was* going on there, it was my job to check it out. Plus, from the map that Candy gave me, there appeared to be a prayer center, the Stations of the Cross, lakes, and other places for reflection...and I desperately needed to clear my head.

My brother, Padraic, had the day off from work and joined me. I picked him up in the morning and off we went. While in the car, we talked about faith. I vented my frustrations from the week, and even told him about my post card dream which, this time, didn't sound as weird when I said it out loud.

Finally, we pulled into Maranatha Spring & Shrine. Our first stop was the prayer center. As we walked in, we saw close to a hundred pictures that people had taken while on the grounds—there were rainbows upon rainbows, everywhere.

There was also an invitation from the Virgin Mary printed on the wall, taken from a message She had given to the visionary: "I extend my invitation...come...to the spring Heaven has given."

Then, there was a prayer for visitors to recite as they enter the property: "I know you have called me to this place...for your purpose....You are inviting me into a deeper personal conversion..."

Padraic looked at me. "This place is your post card," he said. I couldn't believe it. The pictures were just like in my dream! And there was an undeniable connection between the invitation my mother brought to me in a dream, and the real-life invitation the Blessed Mother brought to Elyria. I knew in that moment I was exactly where I was supposed to be—*exactly* where I was supposed to be.

Nothing had ever seemed so clear, actually. I didn't understand *why* I was supposed to be there, but it didn't matter. Finally, the anxiety and stress that I had been feeling throughout the week was gone. Contentment filled my soul.

We took a seat in front of the alcove, and neither of us said five words. Lost in our own thoughts and prayers, we unwound in the unexplainable peace surrounding us. To the right was a statue of the Sacred Heart of Jesus. I stared at the wounds on His hands and began mulling over all the Christian opposition I had encountered throughout the week. I could feel tears welling up in my eyes, and guilt festering in my soul for not defending Him with as much fervor as they used to persecute Him.

I sat there wondering how Jesus was feeling...looking on a world so full of atheism, violence, and selfishness. He gave His life for humanity, and for what? Much of the world now denies the weight of His sacrifice. Even many of His followers (myself included) sit by quietly, as personal "freedom" tries to take over Christianity.

I remembered how alone, out-powered, and scared I felt earlier in the week, and the tears began welling up again. "I can't imagine His sorrow," I thought. A bit embarrassed by my display, I got up from my seat.

Padraic and I began walking around the room, looking at the various shrines, pictures and testimonies. (Apparently miraculous, physical cures have taken place after drinking the water from Maranatha Spring.)

As we approached the statue of Jesus, I again started to get emotional. I got out my camera and took a picture of the statue. To my surprise, the picture that displayed in my camera preview did *not* look like the actual statue in front of me.

The actual statue was looking down towards the floor. It had a chiseled appearance, pale eyes and skin, and a faint smile. The statue in my camera, however, was looking

21

directly at me, not down. He had smooth, flushed skin, glowing blue eyes, and a very sad look about Him. The picture in my camera resembled a real Man, and depicted the kind of sorrow that, moments earlier, I had wondered about.

I stood there, staring at the real and sorrowful face of Jesus Christ in my digital camera. He looked directly at me, and in that moment I knew Him in ways that I hadn't before. His eyes confirmed His sadness. And the way His brows arched, He appeared to be waiting for an answer to something.

In that moment, I remembered my postcard dream, and my mother asking, "Are you going to do it?"

I could hear Jesus asking the question now. Would I defend Him to the opposition? This time, as I looked into His beautiful and sorrowful eyes, I answered without hesitation. "Yes, Lord." I muttered. "I will."

Just then, Padraic came over to me. I showed him the picture in my camera. "What's this?" he said, looking around the room.

"It's that." I said, pointing to the statue in front of us. Padraic's eyes widened.

"Are you serious?" He asked. I nodded. I took another one while Padraic was standing next to me. It turned out exactly the same as the first. In fact, every single picture I took of that statue that day looked real, and very sad.

Standing in our amazement, we were approached by a woman with a strong Jamaican accent, wearing a long wool coat and knitted winter hat. "I thought you might be here," she said. Padraic and I looked at each other. Neither of us had ever seen this woman before. "I was outside," she added. "And suddenly I felt that I had to come in...and here you are." We decided she must work for Holy Love Ministries there at the shrine.

She spoke to us about the apparitions taking place at the grounds, the messages, and Mary's plea for the world to turn back to Christ. But more so, she talked about our lives. She unknowingly talked about everything that Padraic and I had talked about on our ride to the shrine, even those things we silently thought about while sitting in front of the alcove.

At one point, she paused, took my hand, and looked me directly in the eye. "It will be hard...to do all that He asks," she said. "There will be opposition—in our lives, in our work, in our families. But with humility it is possible."

I was speechless. This woman was reading my heart.

"Now go. See the grounds." She said, as she hugged each of us, with a long, warm embrace. And we left the prayer center. Because it was only 15 degrees that day, we drove through the site, and Padraic read about each stop from the directory.

As we approached the rectory and arbor, Padraic read a message from the Virgin Mary given to visionary Maureen Sweeney-Kyle. "My daughter, I am appearing here [above the arbor] as my Son permits it. I desire the people come here every evening at 6:00..." Padraic and I looked at the clock in the car. It was 5:59. By the time we got out of the car and over to the arbor it was exactly 6:00.

We stood staring at a statue of Mary, over the arbor. Just then, we saw a jet in the sky, directly over the statue. It shot upwards leaving its trail behind. A second jet came from the West (shooting towards the East) and crossed over the trail of the first jet. We couldn't believe our eyes. There at 6:00, above the Virgin Mary, was a perfect cross in the sky.

There were other miracles that we experienced that day also. But it was the day as a whole that had the most effect on me. After we left Holy Love Ministries, I went over the events of the day in my mind. And like a puzzle, these separate events came together, and showed me a larger picture at hand.

It was the reported apparitions of the Virgin Mary that eventually drew me to the Holy Love site. But when I got there it was the face of Jesus that I saw, the heart of the crucified Christ that I felt, and the Lord's mercy that manifested in miracles.

It was the Mother of God that invited me. But it was the Son of God who greeted me, and His face will be forever emblazoned on my soul. He revealed Himself to me in a photograph and spoke to me through a Jamaican woman. And by His grace, my life began to take shape. I understood everything that was once confusing: the article, the opposition, and the responsibility I had to both.

When I returned home I framed my miraculous pictures of Jesus. I put a copy above my kitchen sink and openly displayed another copy in my living room, so that anyone who entered would know: this is a house that serves the Lord. I wanted to see the face of my Savior daily, the One who came to me in a desperate moment and revealed to me His peace...the One who made my life new again.

When I started back to work, I put another copy in my office, and I dove back into the article. As I typed, I could see His face—those sad eyes and arched brows—as if still asking, "Are you going to do it?"

And so I did. I typed with fervor, using His teachings in the Gospels as the basis, and His Mother's own words for support. And with the words of the Jamaican woman ringing in my mind, "with humility it is possible," I did not fret over the outcome. I did not worry what others would think of me for writing it, or what the opposition might say in response. I did not tip-toe around any one belief. I did not suppress or exaggerate any piece of information.

Instead, I presented philosophies as they were taught by the first, undivided Church and the evidence as it is made known through science. I used messages from the Virgin Mary found in credible sources. I wrote the way my soul told me it needed to be said...And finally, the article began to flow.

In my Editor's note, I begged our readers (regardless of their position or belief), to open themselves to possibility, and read the article in its entirety. "Because I can tell you from experience," I said. "What we celebrate on Easter *is* true. Christ *is* very much alive today—in the people we meet, the peace we feel, and the miracles we see—and often, it is through His Mother, the Blessed Virgin Mary, that we experience this intimate kind of communion with Him."

CHAPTER 2

"The Tour"

"My grace will travel with you, abounding in every aspect of your journeys on My behalf. Therefore, do not be timid but bold in your response. Surrender to Me. I will bless you."
~Blessed Mother (June 27, 1998)

"The pattern [for the prayer center] is not important. It is the grace given there that will convert many. What have you to fear? My Son is the Master Carpenter." She smiles.
~Blessed Mother (June 25, 1995)

"Please understand, My children, that the layout of this property represents the soul's journey into holiness...The soul is first drawn into My Sorrowful and Immaculate Heart [represented at the Lake of Tears], where he is purged of many of his most flagrant faults. Then he travels along guided by the angels—as is represented on the property by the Lake of Angels. He receives many graces to move deeper into My Heart and into Divine Love, the Heart of My Son. This is represented by Maranatha Spring on the property. Finally, in conformity to the Divine Will of God, he arrives at the Field of Victory, Our United Hearts and the Triumph. Understand that every triumph and victory is surrounded by the Way of the Cross. And thus you have at the back of the property—the Stations of the Cross."
~Blessed Mother (December 12, 1999)

Months later, when the Easter issue of *The Gist* hit the newsstands, I was more than apprehensive about the Apparitions article, and I began to think I shouldn't have run it.

"Oh, this is going to be a disaster," I thought. But after only one day, the phone began ringing off the hook with readers asking for extra copies, and wanting to express their love for it. In fact, one woman recounted a very strong feeling she had while reading it. "I could feel that the Lord is planning to use you in a very big way." She said. "It was a wonderful, wonderful article."

I wasn't sure how to respond, but I was deeply affected by what she said. Since I had returned home from Holy Love Ministries, I felt that I wanted to do more for the Lord. I started to become an entirely different person, with different desires. I even haphazardly told my husband, Tim, that I wanted to write a book about the ancient Faith in the modern world.

Tim looked at me seriously. "Uh, maybe you should concentrate on that busy magazine...before you start on a book project." he admonished.

Yeah, okay. He had a good point. I had two toddlers at home and a very busy workload already. So I dropped it— for now. I didn't have the heart to tell him, though, that the issue wasn't dead completely. I really *did* want to write a book. I wanted it so badly I couldn't get it out of my mind. Day and night it was calling me. Tim was already being overly tolerant with his ever-changing wife, though. So I didn't push the issue any further. Instead, I went to vent to Fr. David, our Pastor at St. Gregory's.

"What can I do for you?" He said, offering me a seat.

"I don't know, Father. I have the *strongest* urge to write a book—something ecumenical, about the ancient faith."

I described to him some of the new fervor I was experiencing and the mysterious "call" I was sensing. "Oh, it's such a *consuming* feeling," I said. "But I don't know what to do with it. I wouldn't even know how to start writing a book... or where on earth I'd find the time."

I rambled on for what seemed like a week. Then, Father took a deep breath. He smiled, "Oh, this is good stuff." He said. "But slow down for a minute."

I laughed. If only I had a nickel for every time someone told me that.

"It's okay that you don't know all the details." He said. "Obviously you don't need to know just yet. So, relax; take it minute by minute, and trust that God will tell you when—and if—it's time to move forward."

He then told me a story about St. Francis De Sales, "who, by the way, is the patron Saint of journalists" he smiled. "St. Francis is most remembered for his writings. He wrote the first spiritual and ecumenical book for the regular lay Christian; and he wrote it at a time when the faith around him was crumbling."

"What a coincidence," I laughed. "My middle name is Francis. I was named after my Grandpa Frank, so it's the man's version (spelled with an i, not an e). I even took Francis as my Confirmation name."

Father smiled. "Hold on for one second," He said. "Let me go get something." He left the room quickly and came back carrying a drawing. "This was given to me, and I never got around to hanging it...maybe because it was supposed to be for you."

It was a modern illustration of St. Francis De Sales. "I want you to have this," he said, handing me the drawing. He also gave me one of St. Francis' books, called the *Introduction to the Devout Life*.

"Thank you so much." I smiled. I admitted to Father that I was feeling much better, that I was okay with the fact that it was not time to move forward with anything, and I left his office contentedly.

A few weeks later, however, it seemed like maybe it was time.

The phone rang. I didn't recognize the number on my caller ID, and usually I don't answer unfamiliar calls when the kids are around (just in case it's a business call and a Barbie fight ensues between my kids).

But for some reason, I answered this one.

"Hi, Stacy." the voice said. "My name is Don Kyle." He was the husband of visionary, Maureen Sweeney-Kyle, from Holy Love Ministries in Elyria, Ohio.

"Why is he calling me?" I thought.

He told me that he and Maureen read the apparitions article in the Spring 2006 issue of *The Gist* magazine. "It was really great," he added. "In fact, Maureen asked the Blessed Mother what She thought of it, and Our Lady said to propagate it."

"Our Lady said what?" I thought. Okay this was weird, but it made perfect sense. After all, I was convinced that it was the Virgin Mary who inspired me to put the article on the schedule that wintry night in my office starring at Wayne Weible's book. Even still...it was hard to wrap my mind around.

"So if you had any extra copies..." Don said.

"Oh, yes, sure." I answered. "My mom and I were actually just planning a trip to Holy Love Ministries. I could bring the magazines with me then, if you'd like."

"That would be great," he said. "We also wanted to talk to you...to see if you would be interested in helping us tell this story."

"Tell this story?" I thought. *"What does that mean? What story—the story of Holy Love Ministries?"* Okay, it was clear now. This poor man dialed the wrong number.

"Well, we don't have to go over it now," he said, breaking the uncomfortable silence.

"Of course," I added. "I'd be happy to help with whatever you need."

"Okay, great," he said. "We'll talk about it when you come."

"That sounds good." I said. He gave me his phone number and told me to call him to confirm a couple days before I came. I told him I was looking forward to it and we hung up.

"Well...that was weird," I said to myself. And things were only getting weirder.

A few moments later, Candy Kelly stopped by to see me. We had kept in touch after she introduced me to Holy Love Ministries, and we were becoming good friends.

"I have a message for you," she said.

"Come on in," I smiled. "A message?"

"I was at Maranatha Spring yesterday, and a woman named Mary Ann, who is one of the visionary's close friends, said to me: 'if you see Stacy, tell her it was the Blessed Mother in her postcard dream, not her birth mother. And if she's confused, tell her to read Wayne Weible.'" Candy shrugged her shoulders. " I don't know who Wayne Weible is or what that means. I'm just relaying the message."

I nodded. I knew well who Wayne Weible was. He was the author of the book on Medjugorje that I found in my old briefcase.

"Wayne Weible wrote about the Medjugorje apparitions," I explained. "I have one of his books."

"Oh, perfect!" she said. "What's so special about him?"

"I don't know..." I admitted. "Our Lady asked him to write his first book. He wrote a lot of books on Medjugorje though. He's one of the main proponents of it."

"Well, maybe you're supposed to write about Holy Love." She suggested.

"Well, it's funny you should say that. Don Kyle just called me and asked if I would be interested in helping them tell their story."

"You've been feeling like you should write a book," Candy reminded me.

"Yes," I said, "but I feel like it is supposed to be something *ecumenical*...I certainly haven't been sensing a book on Marian apparitions."

We chatted for a few more minutes about the confusing turn of events. "You'll understand it soon." She said, and gave me a hug. "I have to get going. But have a safe trip when you go. And call me!"

The day of our trip came quickly, and I had an enormous amount to do, at home and at work. Normally, it would not have been time to head off on a spiritual pilgrimage...But, this was not a normal situation. I was so drawn to Maranatha Spring & Shrine that nothing on my little to-do list could compare to what was stirring hungrily inside me. I couldn't distinguish it myself, and I didn't dare try to explain it to anyone else, but I made every effort to get myself to Elyria, OH one way or the other.

Luckily, things just fell into place. My next door neighbor was able to babysit the kids for the day until Tim came home from work. The weather was perfect—70 and sunny. I packed a small lunch, some empty water jugs, and my camera; then went to pick up my mother, brothers, sister-in-law, aunt and cousin. Overall, the morning went rather swimmingly. (This you have to understand is a miracle in itself for my family. In fact, it might actually have been the first time ever—in 30 years—that a smooth, timely departure had occurred.)

When we pulled into the driveway I noticed an older man, clean cut, in a light golf shirt and khaki pants, walking towards us. He waved and I realized it was him.

"Don?" I said cheerily.

"Hey, Stace!" he said. He smiled a candid smile that seemed to reveal his whole nature. It was light and gentle. I couldn't help but to smile back at him. He seemed to be about 60 or so, but there was a peace about him that made me wonder if he felt a great deal younger than even that. We shook hands and I introduced him to my family.

He shook their hands, asked how our drive was and where everyone was from. Then he began to talk about Maranatha Spring & Shrine.

"This shrine is exactly how the Blessed Mother requested it." He said. "Our Lady tells us what to do—what to build and where to build it—and we do it. It's been that way from the beginning."

He led us over to the driveway and pulled around a few golf carts. "I'll give you a tour of the site first, and then Maureen would like to meet with you, if you have time. She's not here right now though."

I nodded. He took us to the prayer center first, and showed us a large book, several inches thick or so. Inside, were thousands of letters from pilgrims describing the miracles they experienced either at Maranatha Spring or after they returned home with the water from the Spring. There were testimonies of physical healings, rosaries turning to gold, spiritual conversions and unexplainable peace.

Don also showed us some of the pictures that were hanging up, some of the other miracles that people had captured on film. One in particular caught my eye. It was a photo someone had taken of the white statue of the Blessed Mother at the prayer center. In the photo, the statue looked like a real woman with flesh-toned skin...and She was stepping out of the alcove, toward the photographer. It was truly phenomenal.

I was then drawn over to the statue of Jesus. My mom whispered, "Is this the one you took a picture of last time?" I nodded. "It doesn't look anything like your picture." She said. I nodded again.

Looking at the statue I felt like I was somewhere else. The eyes of the statue were so captivating, so alluring. It felt so good to be back at the Shrine.

We walked by the statues of St. Therese, the little Flower and St. John Vianney—two patron Saints of the property. Then we came to the apparition room, a small room off to the side where Maureen sits during the rosary services. Inside, there was a painting of Jesus on the wall and I couldn't take my eyes off it. It was the most amazing rendition of Him that I had ever seen, and I thought the same thing the last time I visited the site. There was just something about that image...something I couldn't put my finger on, that had affected me in a very powerful way. Don pointed to the painting.

"We bought this picture in California," he said. "Maureen and I were at a religious shop, when, suddenly, she stopped and pointed to this picture. She said this is almost exactly how Jesus looks when He appears to her."

Don then showed us a small glass box on the wall. Inside was a strand of dark hair. He explained that this piece of hair was found after an apparition and that it was actually a strand of the Blessed Mother's hair. He said many miracles have been reported by pilgrims who have touched the box. I began to wonder about the possibility of a Heavenly being having real hair... and how or why a strand would fall out, to be left on earth.

Quickly it dawned on me that if the Blessed Mother was assumed into Heaven—both *body* and soul—it is actually very feasible for a strand of Her hair to be left behind. And if the Lord was truly all-merciful, He would allow it to fall out for *our* good, so that we might have one more means by which to attain the unending grace He offers us through His Mother.

"There have been many miracles associated with this, as well," Don said, "many physical healings."

He led us back outside to the golf carts, and we followed him to a small teardrop-shaped lake called the Lake of Tears. It was beautiful, just beautiful. White gravel, neatly kept landscaping, and a statue of the Blessed Mother. There were seven white signs placed around the water, with meditations written on them. Each meditation described a sorrow that the Blessed Mother experienced in Her life—sorrows still alive and well in Her Heart today.

"Our Lady has said that this is one of her favorite places on earth." Don explained.

After a while, we drove a short distance to a slightly larger lake, just up the road. This one was called the Lake of Angels. "The Blessed Mother told us that She has placed one angel from each of the nine choirs of angels around this lake, Don explained. "She also said that the first time a person comes to Maranatha Spring they receive another angel—in addition to their guardian angel—who will follow them home and assist them throughout life."

It was a very comforting thought, that in that moment we were surrounded by so many heavenly beings, and that several of them would go so far as to follow us home. "Our Lady said that we could name our angel whatever we wanted," Don added. "What was most important was that we called upon this angel in our times of need."

I thought of what I would name mine. Immediately Frank came to mind. I'm not sure why—maybe because Francis had played such a significant role in my life in recent months. I chuckled to myself at the thought of it—an angel named Frank. It seemed fitting nonetheless.

Next to the lake was a very small out-building, called the Chapel of Angels. Inside, there were hundreds of additional testimonies hung up on the walls—various letters from people who had experienced miracles as a result of drinking (or rinsing in) the spring water. Some were simply because of making the pilgrimage. There was even a large newspaper clipping that featured the unexplainable healing of several people who recently visited the Shrine. Don told us of other testimonies that he knew of. We listened in utter amazement.

Back in the golf carts, we followed the winding road deeper into the property. Don pointed to the statue of St. Michael the Archangel on the right, off in the distance across a large field.

To the left was the Field of Victory and Maranatha Spring. It was a simple, manual water pump sticking out of the ground at the entrance to an enormous field. Next to it, there was a sign displaying a message from the Blessed Mother. It read: "Joyfully, I reveal to you today that the waters of Maranatha are as the Lourdes of this continent. They are comparable in healing grace, both in body and soul...Therefore; you can propagate it with much faith and hope." (May 31, 1995)

Don and I stood off to the side and began to discuss the water at length. "There is so much grace here," He stared. "So many people come seeking physical cures...and some find them. But others are disappointed when they don't. It's sad, really. They are so consumed with *their* will—with getting healed—that they forget to consider what is *God's* will for them. Sometimes God pours out a different kind of grace here at this site—the kind of grace that gives a person strength to endure, or enlightenment to understand their situation. Some miss out on that grace though, looking for a healing. We wish that everyone would be healed, but that's not always God's Will."

After filling up our jugs, we loaded them into the golf carts and drove further into the Field of the United Hearts (the Field of Victory), where there were statues of the Sacred Heart of Jesus and the Immaculate Heart of Mary.

This statue of Jesus was different from the one in the prayer center. This one was solid white and a 'kingly' look about it. Don explained that it was here, in the United Hearts field, that midnight apparitions were held. "Everyone gathers together here, to pray the rosary. And at some point during our prayer, The Blessed Mother appears. This field is just filled with people," he said. "It's truly something. Thousands of people come from all over the world."

What a remarkable thought: a field full of thousands of people, all praying the rosary together. At that, we drove to the back of the field, to a statue of Padre Pio, one of the other Patron Saints of the ministry. We then headed towards a large, white cross that stood at an opening in a line of trees.

"Here we have the Way of the Cross," Don pointed from the golf cart. We drove into the woods, following a footpath, obviously well-worn by many pilgrims. It weaved through large, mature trees, where every so often there stood a beautiful plaque illustrating a specific point of the Lord's Passion. "Even this," Don said, "is designed exactly how Our Lady wanted it. She showed us where each station was to be and how the path would weave through these trees."

As we drove out of the woods, we arrived at a statue of St. Joseph in front of another (smaller) lake. We stopped the carts and all got out. The sun was glistening off the water, and warming my face. The air was quiet and still. We too, stood quiet and still in the moment, as it seemed to be the last shrine on our pilgrimage...

But it was by no means, the end of our Maranatha experience.

CHAPTER 3

"The Resolution"

"Heaven holds an affinity for those who venerate My Dolors (sorrows). This is why special and unusual graces will be given. The Shrine of your Heavenly Mother's Sorrows will be a site of favor. The water coming into the Lake of Tears is My tears. This water will bring special consolation to mothers who sorrow for their wayward children...My affection and presence is always at Maranatha Spring, the Lake of Tears and the holy Stations of the Cross."
(September 8, 1997)

"At My Lake of Tears, I will alleviate the afflicted, make steadfast the wavering heart, and console the downtrodden. What more then do you need or desire? I am blessing you."
(September 16, 1997)

"My messenger, do you see the little bee gathering pollen from the flowering tree outside? The bee is like many and all of the pilgrims who come to the prayer site. They gather what information and graces they can from the mission. Like the bee who returns to the hive to make honey, the pilgrims return home, hopefully to allow the message to bear fruit in their lives. The bee does not have to fly to any other source of pollen. That tree has enough blossoms to satisfy him over and over. So too, the pilgrim can find everything he needs at this apparition site...Grace abounds here...Just as our little bee is completely satisfied with his source of pollen, the pilgrim who comes to Maranatha will be satisfied in his needs. I have withheld nothing from those who come...Make this known."
~Jesus (May 3, 2001)

While we stood in front of the St. Joseph shrine, Don received a phone call. It was Maureen.

"Maureen is home now," he said. "If you want, we could go meet with her?" Again, I just nodded...a little apprehensively. I mean, I wanted to meet with her, but I had such mixed emotions. I didn't feel like I, personally, should be meeting with a woman that has almost daily contact with our Lord and the Blessed Mother.

We drove to their residence and Don led us into their private chapel. He went to get Maureen while we waited. A few minutes later, she came in. I stood up. She smiled a very gentle smile, softly said hello, and we shook hands. I was utterly amazed at how...how....*normal* she was.

I don't know what I was expecting her to be like, but she was simple and sweet. I guessed she was about sixty with short hair (blond still), wearing regular khaki shorts and a button down shirt. She seemed to be quite normal in appearance...though I don't dare call her "common". In her meekness and humility she radiated a very warm spirit, a genuine friendliness. She made me feel, surprisingly, comfortable near her.

After introductions we all sat down. She sat directly across from me. While the others talked, she discreetly leaned over and handed me a folded index card. Confused, I looked at it. Then I looked up at her. She was smiling. In perfect cursive handwriting the card read:

6/16/06   Jesus

"I welcome Stacy back to the property. I will embrace her heart and her efforts to make this site known."

"It's from today," she whispered. It was a message that she received from Jesus that morning. I sat staring at it, tears welling up in my eyes and love surging throughout my being. I felt a million miles away from this planet.

My mom leaned over and read the card.

"Stace...." She gasped. She was stunned.

Surprisingly, however, I was not. Certainly, I never expected to get a hand-written message from the Lord. But what was written on that index card was not a new revelation to me. Rather, it was confirmation of the message I felt deep in my heart the last time I visited the Shrine.

That first day, when I looked deep into His face in my digital camera, I heard those words in the silence of my soul, and I continued to hear them upon my return home. The graces followed me back to my regular life...changing the way I viewed almost everything around me. I knew that He would embrace my efforts then, writing the article, and that He would continue to do so for as long as I put forth the effort.

The handwritten words staring back at me were simply confirmation that I was, in fact, hearing Him. It assured me that I could listen to my soul with confidence that it was Heaven who was inspiring me and strengthening me. How grateful I was for this confirmation. How overcome I was with love for Him.

"You are so good, Lord," I thought, *"so very, very good."*

Later, Maureen spoke up and commented on the apparitions report in *The Gist*. "It was beautiful," she said. Then, she asked if I would be interested in telling the story of Maranatha Spring and Shrine.

Without hesitation I answered, "Yes, of course, whatever you need." It was strange, really. The words just fell out of my mouth. It was as though they were coming directly from my heart—and so quickly, as if they had been awaiting the question. I felt such an excitement about it...and yet, I knew nothing of what it might require.

"Maybe Candy was right," I thought. *"Maybe this is the book that I have wanted to write."*

The conversation of our group veered onto other topics. Don and my family were doing most of the chatting.

My mother recognized this, however, and asked Maureen if she would like to talk to me in private, away from all of them.

I looked at her, embarrassed. She's fearless that mother of mine. She'll ask anyone, anything, without reservation. I, however, am more comfortable in the quiet, wallflower position. Maureen agreed, though, and we went inside their residence. I couldn't believe my mom had asked her that...but, I *was* glad to have the time to speak with her alone.

We didn't talk about anything specific, but I got a very specific feeling about her. This woman was as shy as I was, no doubt. Clearly, she was not in this for the recognition. She wasn't fabricating apparitions to bring attention to herself. In fact, it was obvious to me that she wasn't completely comfortable with all the attention—even after all these years.

This caused me to realize the great sacrifice this woman has made. The lives of all those people who have been converted by miracles at the Shrine—myself included—have been changed because this woman said "yes" to what the Lord and Blessed Mother asked her to do: "make this known."

How easy it would have been for a shy, timid woman to stick her head in the sand and let the world carry on around her. Instead, she stepped forward as an American

46

visionary in a world that would no doubt ridicule her. I felt such gratitude for that. I knew how hard it must have been for her to spread this message, given her personality. But what I didn't know was that her unease in the spotlight was only a small fraction of what she had endured.

"I guess it's time to tell the story," She said. "And oh, what an interesting story it is—how this shrine came to be and the resistance we've come up against. No one is writing a book on it yet. So, if *you're* interested in doing it…"

I felt deep in my soul I was supposed to do it. I didn't know how, or when, or what it would even be about. But I knew it had to be done. "I am definitely willing to do it." I told Maureen.

"Good." She smiled.

After a bit of chatting, she walked me to the door. I hugged her tightly and thanked her for all that she had done.

"You too, kiddo," she said, and returned the embrace. In that moment I knew this would be the start of a beautiful friendship. I felt connected to her on a spiritual level, united in our love for Jesus, the Blessed Mother, and for this place.

As I walked out, I noticed the rest of my group had already left the chapel and were waiting outside with Don, who had one more place to take us. This time we got in our cars and headed over to the book store. It was a small, unassuming building full of books, rosaries, prayer cards, and other items to aid one's spiritual journey.

Don took one of almost every book from the shelves and placed them in my hands. Most were organized compilations of the messages that have been given to Maureen. But a few others were histories of the Blessed Mother.

"You'll need these," he smiled.

Then I saw one particular book that stuck out from the shelves. It was a book of Marian Sermons, written by none other than St. Francis De Sales. I smiled. The irony set my heart at ease.

Don told the woman working at the checkout counter that the books were taken care of. I thanked him and we agreed to get together in a few weeks. "It was nice meeting all of you," he said to my family. "Enjoy your stay at the Shrine today and have a safe trip home."

After he left, we began to go back through the property, spending more time at each shrine. While at the Lake of Tears I began to re-think my situation.

"Would I have time to write a book," I thought. *"in addition to managing the magazine and being a wife and a mother? Even if I did find the time, what in the world made me think I was qualified for such a task?*

I started to get a little anxious, trying to wrap my mind around what was being asked of me. It seemed as though the request should have been for someone else.

"Am I the right person for this, Lord?" I prayed. *"I'm just thirty years old. And it's not like I have a lifetime of theology, wisdom, or experience to support what may be required of me. I don't even have a college degree."* (As if He didn't know.)

I recounted my college experience...what a mess I was then. I couldn't decide on a major. I couldn't stay away from the party scene. I couldn't drag myself to class, and naturally, I couldn't' convince the institution to let me stay after a three-term failing GPA. Yes, that's right, I flunked out, after only two and a half years, and went through a period of even greater self-destruction after that.

Later, however, I got lucky (or rather, I was blessed). A local magazine was hiring, and asked me to write a pre-employment essay instead of checking my transcripts. So I landed myself a job where I eventually worked my way up.

But now... here I was, face-to-face with an opportunity to write for the Lord and our Blessed Mother. I had screwed up so many times before, blown so many other opportunities, that I thought for sure there was a more qualified candidate out there somewhere—someone who had remained faithful to Them, who knew Marian theology, or at least had a college degree in journalism for crying out loud.

In my mind I felt unprepared for this task. In my heart, I felt unworthy to write this story. But it was precisely because of my heart—and the love I had for Jesus—that made me *want* to do it anyway, in spite of my inadequacies.

"But is that selfish?" I wondered. *"Wouldn't the book be more effective, and bring Him greater glory, if someone more qualified did it?"*

I squatted down by the side of the lake and stuck my hands in the cool water. My palms were facing down. I wiggled my fingers slowly, as though typing on a keyboard. Instantly, swarms of fish swam to my fingers and sat at the tips of them. There were big fish and small fish, light fish and dark fish. I wiggled my fingers again and the fish stayed there, watching me. More swam over. Their mouths were puckered, pointed upwards toward the top of the water, as though looking desperately for food.

Obviously, the fish were used to people gathering around this lake, and that's why they were not afraid. But it was still a profound moment for me, as I recalled the gospel of Matthew (4:19).

Jesus begins His ministry (age 30) and calls His first disciples—four fishermen on the Sea of Galilee, who by the way, weren't religious leaders or rabbis. They were the lowly, the uneducated. "Follow me." Jesus said to them. "And I will make you fishers of men."

I smiled, thinking of the disciples and watching the fish, so closely resembling mankind...big fish, small fish, light fish, dark fish. I smiled at the coincidence—that my fingers moved as though typing and a multitude of fish swarmed near them.

Clearly, Our Lady was asking me to just follow Jesus, to make this place known. There is a multitude of desperate and starving souls in this world, who are looking for spiritual food, and I knew from personal experience that the Lord could feed them and nourish them, here at Maranatha Spring & Shrine.

I knew that their emptiness could be filled at the Spring, their dryness restored at the lakes. I knew lost souls could find their way by walking that footpath in the woods. And I knew brokenness—even the most desperate kind— could be sewn back together with a relic of Our Lady's hair.

The fish staring at me from that water were gripping my heart because of what they represented...souls. I thought of the disciples who immediately dropped their nets and followed Him. And I realized something.

The Blessed Mother invited me to this site. She shed grace on my soul, and asked me to make this journey with Her Son. My mouth said yes, and I walked to the starting line.

But there I stood: my head down, paralyzed at the thought of my inadequacies, unable to take even one step forward.

It was time for me to make a decision. Like the disciples I, too, needed to drop my net—my insecurities, doubts, and concerns for time. I could feel Our Lady gently urging me. I was to be a fisher of men by making this place known. I myself had nothing to give these poor fish before me; but I had great confidence that the souls who would swarm to Maranatha would be fulfilled with spiritual food that the Lord Himself has made available here, through His Mother.

"Okay," I thought. *"I will do it."*

There, at the Lake of Tears, I had made my resolution to begin the journey. I was not entirely sure *how* I would do it, even *if* I could do it, but I gave my fiat. Somewhere in my heart I found the strength to want to try.

It was just like Our Lady's words to Maureen, "At the Lake of Tears I will alleviate the afflicted, *make steadfast the wavering heart*, and console the downtrodden." (September 16, 1997)

I stood up and found my mom standing behind me, smiling. This was amazing. My mother had come to the Shrine with a heart pierced with sorrow. She was troubled by a situation that had been dragging on for many years— something that had been weighing heavy on her soul and, despite her prayers, seemed to be growing worse the last few months. She spent much of the day in tears over it. But there, at the Lake of Tears, she too stood smiling at a statue of the Sorrowful Mother. We began to walk toward the Lake of Angels.

"I haven't seen you smile all day." I whispered to her.

She beamed back at me. "I gave it to Mary. She took it from me, back at that Lake..." She sighed deeply. "She has it now, and I don't have to worry anymore."

She was walking with a lighter step and brighter eyes.

"Amazing..." I thought. My sorrowing mother, unable to handle the pain in her heart was relieved at the Lake of Tears. She was a true example of a hungry soul fed by grace.

It brought to mind a message from September 8, 1997. Our Lady came to Maureen as the Sorrowful Mother. She said: "My angel, I come in praise of Jesus. Today, I invite you to understand that My victory will be one of love and of sorrow. My victory will come through tears for the many who will be lost. This is why, in these times, heaven holds an affinity for those who venerate My Dolors. This is why special and unusual graces will be given. The Shrine of your Heavenly Mother's Sorrows will be a site of favor. The water coming into the Lake of Tears is My tears. This water will bring special consolation to mothers who sorrow for their wayward children. For today, it is the good who suffer and the converted who are persecuted. I understand the pain of a mother's heart and I have requested this grace from My Beloved Son. Continually there are many angels in attendance with Me at this Lake of Tears. They are carrying petitions to Heaven as I desire. You will begin to see many images there."

CHAPTER 4

"The Path"

"My brothers and sisters, put the household of your hearts in order with the broom of Holy Love; for when I return and reign over My Kingdom, which is to come, those who will be seated at My feet are those consecrated to...Holy Love."
~Jesus (June 12, 1998)

"To live in Holy Love is to live the two great commandments— love God above all else and neighbor as self. But I offer you even more than that: to be perfected in Holy Love is to be purified in God's Will. Thus, you are drawn into Divine Love and union with the Trinity. This is Heaven on earth, the Kingdom to come, the New Jerusalem."
~Jesus (March 11, 1999)

"You will have courage and perseverance if your hearts are prepared in Holy and Divine Love...Sweep the household of your soul clean. Shed the debris from your life. Allow the Flame of Divine Love to consume you—embrace you."
~Jesus (December 5, 1999)

"Dear children, please understand that as I lead you along the path of Holy Love, I am leading you along the path of salvation. For no one enters paradise who does not love."
~Blessed Mother (March 9, 1994)

I returned home from Maranatha Spring and immediately dove into the books of messages Don had given me. I was curious about the name, Holy Love Ministries, which seemed to be thematic throughout the Shrine...even the way the Blessed Mother appeared to Maureen—as Mary, Refuge of Holy Love. What was this "Holy Love" so often spoken of and why was it so common at this site?

As soon as I opened the books, I couldn't put them down...even with all the housework I had to do—and oh-boy, was there a lot of it.

As my family had grown busier, running from one event or function to the next, my house had simultaneously grown dirtier. We had been rushing in and out, dropping things wherever they fell, eating a quick snack and then hurriedly tossing the dish in the sink before dashing out the door for the next occasion. It seemed I was not home long enough to devote any real attention to housekeeping, but just long enough to grow discouraged with the scene: several tornado-swept rooms, a mountain of dirty laundry, and a sink full of crusty dishes.

Ugh. Despair had set in. I began to think it was an impossible achievement: managing an orderly house with our kind of lifestyle. I even tried to convince myself that sadly, I will never have a clean house for as long as I have a job, young kids living at home, or a residence in the same town as so many family and close friends—for whom there are so many blessed events that we wish to attend.

Despite all this, I sat down with several books from Don and decided to ignore the squalor. But while reading through the messages, I realized that my attitude regarding my dirty house was quite similar to my attitude regarding my dirty soul. I had fallen prey to the modern deception that holiness (like my household cleanliness) is an unrealistic aspiration and altogether unattainable.

It seems our culture has assigned "holiness" to those select few who are called to religious vocations, or the homebound who have extensive time for prayer and meditation.

It was not for me, though. I was a young, busy mom living in the "real world". And as I got busier, running from one event or function to the next, my soul naturally got dirtier—a little more tainted and a little more desensitized to my surroundings. It wasn't my fault. It was the *world...* or so I told myself.

I just did like everyone else: I rushed in and out, hurriedly tossing God aside to dash out to the next occasion...not home, or still, long enough to devote any real attention to prayer and soul-keeping, but just long enough to grow impatient and irritated by the people around me.

I had convinced myself that it was okay, though. I'm only human, and it's just not humanly possible to be "holy" while living day-to-day in this demanding—and not very pious—world.

But there I was, reading a book full of messages from the Holy and Blessed Mother of God, and it dawned on me: this too was a copout. I was ignoring the squalor in my soul, and the Virgin Mary said to take heed. She had come to Maranatha Spring with a call—an invitation—and not just for pastors and priests as I had thought, but for *all* people, of all faiths. Perhaps this was the ecumenical book I was sensing.

She told Maureen, "I desire, my daughter, that you most clearly understand that My appearances to you are all-encompassing. I do not come for a small or certain select group. I come to convert the world..." (July 26, 1996)

Over and over again, Our Lady stressed in no uncertain terms, that each one of us is called to holiness regardless of our vocation, our profession, our age, how many kids we have or don't have.

Looking around my house, now closely resembling a war zone, I thought how similar it was to my cluttered soul—so full of junk and hard to look at. I realized the gravity of the matter. My soul was a war zone—a sought-after territory for both my Lord and His enemy (who I had probably, though inadvertently, given an upper hand to in my apathy).

"To choose other than holiness is to choose Satan," Mary said. (June 17, 1993)

Through these messages, Our Lady unveiled the one true path we are to walk. It's the road that God Himself designed, to lead us home to Him. I found myself spiritually standing before it, and I sighed deeply.

"But, me? Holy?" I thought. I was faithful, sure, but I certainly didn't consider myself *holy*. I sighed again. *"I wouldn't even know how to start such an endeavor."*

Glancing back at the book, I found the Blessed Mother had an answer even for that. And I understood that, just like my despairingly dirty house was actually cleanable (with some work) so it was with my soul, thanks to Jesus for what He did on the Cross. "The only thing that keeps a soul from holiness is free will," Our Lady said. (July 29, 1993)

This surprised me because I had always assumed it was my current vocation that kept me from holiness. Somewhere along the line I developed the notion that holiness came with an in-depth knowledge of Scripture, ministry involvement, extensive ritual, etc. And so I took a defeatist position. I accepted that, as a young mother with no extra time to devote to such matters, I was not holy, and probably wouldn't become holy, until maybe I was elderly— when I had the time to work on it, and the urgency to drive such efforts.

But here, the Virgin Mary was saying something entirely different: I *could* actually foster piety in this busy world, and I didn't need to get a new job, have total seclusion, or wait until my kids leave the house to do it. In fact, I could attain it here and now, by remembering just two simple things.

The first thing, ironically, was remembering the here and now. The Blessed Mother said you need to be conscious of the present moment. The second thing was to choose love in each present moment...an act Jesus Himself stressed in the Gospels.

The religious leaders asked Jesus which commandment was the greatest. Jesus told them simply, "This is the first...you must love the Lord your God with all your heart, with all your soul, with all your mind and with all your strength. The second is this: You must love your neighbor as yourself. There is no commandment greater than these." (Mark 12:28-31).

It was as simple as that. If I wanted to attain holiness, I had to adhere to these commands: to love God above all else and my neighbor as myself. These commands were given to us by Jesus Himself. Therefore, they were holy. This was very enlightening for me: the fact that expressing love is—and always has been—a *holy* act.

This gave me hope that I wasn't doomed to be unholy my whole life. In fact, just by being conscious of the present moment—and by choosing to love in each of my moments—I could grow in (and eventually perfect) personal holiness.

All I had to do was use my free will for God. I had to *choose* words, thoughts, and actions that better express love for God and my neighbor. In all decisions, I simply had to ask myself, "Which way best shows love?" And minute by minute, I could find myself taking giant steps toward holiness.

What's more, the Blessed Mother said that in this simple little facet of time lies the soul's very salvation. "I desire you be sanctified (made holy), My dear children, always in the present moment, for here is your salvation." (July 29, 1995)

At first, that sounded absurd to me—that a brief little moment can have such everlasting effects—but the more I read the messages, the more I realized the enormous depth of what She was saying.

Holy Love is the very foot path of salvation, cleared one step (one moment) at a time. It cannot be hurried. It cannot be cleared by any other way. You cannot skip over sections of the journey or teleport to the end.

In the present moment, with one right choice, we can use our free will to choose God's Will, which is simply to love. If we fail, and we don't choose to love, we have the very next present moment to repent and begin anew.

"...Sin is committed only in the present moment," Our Lady told Maureen. "Therefore, consecrate your hearts to holiness (August 11, 1994)... My Son will not be satisfied with half choices or indecisions. These are choices against Holy Love. This is why people must see how important it is to love in the present moment. When My Son comes He will not look at what was in your hearts in the past, or what might be in the future. He will look into your heart in the present." (January 16, 1995)

"Hmmm..." I thought. *"It did make sense."* By living in the present moment, we don't dwell on past moments or worry about future moments. Instead, we trust past moments to God's mercy and forgiveness, and we trust future moments to His provision and protection. Guilt over the past and anxiety over the future are often the very things that drive us to choose *against* love anyway.

"When Satan takes your will into the past, he conjures up grudges," Mary said, "which is always contrary to God's Will and Holy Love. To willfully think of the future allows Satan to bring up worries." (October 4, 1993)

Going into the past is like taking steps backwards, trying to re-walk old steps. Going into the future is like going nowhere. It is being paralyzed, motionless with fear. No progress is made, rather time is lost.

Living Holy Love in every present moment helps us not to slip up as often. It helps us remain more grounded in faith. But more so, "it is the way out of every situation that would destroy your peace." Our Lady said. (June 20 1994)

For example, when we give of ourselves, we give in the present, only out of love for God and our neighbor. Then there is no resentment over our charity. We know it's the right decision, and we don't look back.

When we work, we do all things with a loving heart, even those things that require much effort and even discomfort. But we don't keep a scorecard tallying these labors; we don't track what is due us because of our efforts. We are not doing these things for future reward, but for love.

Similarly, when we are tested, we look for the choice to love God first and then neighbor. Then there is no anxiety over decisions, no confusion as to the path we should take. In the end, there is no regret, no expectation, no disappointment, and no fear. There is only love and thus, as the Virgin Mary said, there is only peace. What's more, there is progress.

Holy Love is a one-way path, so it is also the direction. It's straight-forward. Anything other than Holy Love is self-love, which takes you away from the goal of holiness.

While reading these messages, I decided that living in the present moment was a perfect way to stay on track, but something still wasn't sitting well with me. I was doubting and wrestling with this in my mind. I kept thinking of it from Jesus' perspective. And I wondered, *"What's the big deal about one little moment? Why would Jesus prefer I give him one moment versus my whole life?"*

To me, it didn't seem to be enough. One little moment didn't seem to be an adequate offering for people serious about their faith or becoming holy. I mean, if I was *really* committed to Him then wouldn't it stand to reason that I should be able to commit more than just this present moment to Him? I mean, if on our wedding day, my husband didn't promise me more than just that moment, I'd be extremely hurt.

I started doubting the whole theory. Then, a simple question entered my train of thought, very slowly and distinctly. *"What exactly is the present moment, if there is no past or future to relate it to?"* I heard the answer in my soul. *"It's eternity."*

It's a moment of complete focus and consciousness, repeating over and over. It's not governed by what has been (past) or what will be (future). It's a continual renewal of commitment and love to Jesus—and His continual response of Love and Mercy in return.

In the present moment, there is a vibrant relationship with God and all the people He has put in our lives. It's a relationship that doesn't grow stale or become lukewarm from being set aside. My decision to change my lifestyle and live in Holy Love—that was my "big" commitment to God, like my husband's big decision to change his lifestyle with a marriage proposal.

By giving the Lord my every moment, I don't lessen the commitment, rather I strengthen the relationship. It's similar to the way I can strengthen my marriage by giving my husband my love in *every moment*—not just assuming he already knows I love him because of the commitment (the vows) I once made, several years ago.

By giving God my *every* moment, I invite Him to take each step with me. Here is the secret to becoming holy and truly walking with the Lord—not just on Sundays, not just in morning prayer, but all day, *every* day.

What hope there is in the present moment! A soul (much like my despairingly dirty house) can actually become clean—holy—in the present moment. I closed the book of messages from Our Lady and was so grateful for Her words. They brought such clarity and hope to my soul. In that present moment, I looked around at my filthy house and decided to get to work on the squalor, one little moment at a time.

"I guess I'll start with this sink full of dishes," I sighed.

CHAPTER 5

"The Entryway"

"My words to you will be beacons of light that lay bare the path of holiness...Few will choose to follow. All are called. Hasten to understand that to which you are summoned."
~Blessed Mother (September 23, 1993)

"My Son's Heart always holds supremacy over my Immaculate Heart. But in depicting Our Hearts as United, He shows the world that Divine Love is only approachable through Holy Love. Living in the Divine Will is attainable by living in Holy Love. Therefore, it is mankind's 'yes' to Holy Love that unites him completely to God. The greater the commitment to holiness in this way, the deeper his union with God."
~Blessed Mother (September 26, 1996)

"Therefore, see and understand, that the United Hearts of Jesus and Mary represents union between Holy and Divine Love. This is the union Jesus wants with each soul. This is why He sends Me, so that I am able to lead you into union with Him through My own Heart. You must pray for unyielding hearts who threaten their own salvation by refusing to pursue this path of salvation. You will please make this known."
~Blessed Mother (February 9, 1997)

Since the apparitions article, more and more people from my hometown, were approaching me—in the grocery store, after Mass, in the post office. They felt the need to share with me some of the great miracles that they experienced after visiting Maranatha Spring. How blessed I felt to see and hear the gratitude of a soul touched by grace!

I was so excited about this endeavor that I quickly called Don and Maureen to set up a time to get together. We scheduled our first interview for the middle of July. But as I thought more about this, it became a little daunting. What started in a dream, turned into a road trip, and has since become a call to assist in Heaven's efforts to lead souls. It was overwhelming.

Also, there was something I forgot to mention about my first trip to Ohio that wintry day with my brother. What should have been a two-hour drive, took more than three hours. What should have been a straight-forward highway journey, resulted in more than an hour on back roads, little neighborhoods and strange towns. My poor brother was patient with me... but let's face it: I had no idea where I was going. And this was before the days of smart phones and Siri.

I had never been to the shrine before. I didn't know what I was looking for, and I didn't spend enough time figuring it out ahead of time. As I thought about this new endeavor (writing this book) I realized how similar it was to that trip. I felt as though I had set out on the journey, without having any idea where I was headed. So, before I meet with Don and Maureen, I decided I should probably familiarize myself with the messages a little more.

So, I dove into that pile of books from Don. There were two thick books that contained the bulk of the messages. On the front covers of both books, there was the same image—two fiery hearts—which I knew from the Shrine was called the "United Hearts".

To be honest though: at first, the image was a little too much for me. I didn't understand what it meant. It just seemed weird—you know, it being fiery hearts and all.

I knew that the image of the United Hearts represented the Sacred Heart of Jesus (the big heart) united to the Immaculate Heart of Mary (the smaller heart)...but honestly, at this point in my life, all I really knew about the Sacred Heart of Jesus was that there was a parish in Erie named after it. As far as the Immaculate Heart of Mary goes...well, I could only assume it had something to do with Her Immaculate Conception—though I didn't know for sure.

It's embarrassing to say, since I am a cradle Catholic and went to Catholic schools, but I knew nothing more about these two symbols. Why hearts? Why fire? What did they represent? The messages talked often about these "United Hearts", an entire field was named after them at the Shrine. The image was displayed in the prayer center, medals and scapulars were available at the gift shop. But what did they symbolize?

I decided I should back up a little. If I was going to understand the bulk of these messages, I would first need to understand these Hearts. And thanks to an article by author and Marian priest, Monsignor Arthur B. Calkins, it all started to make sense.

"...The 'heart' is a shorthand way of speaking about the whole person," he said, "with special emphasis on [the person's] interiority."

70

It was like a light went on. People often use clichés that follow this same kind of 'Catholic' thinking. The best example is, "let's have a heart to heart". When someone asks to have a 'heart to heart' conversation with you, they simply want to have an intimate, honest, no-holds-barred talk with you. They want to understand you—your innermost being—because they want to draw closer to you.

So what is the heart? The heart is not only the place of emotions. It's the hub of the person, command central, if you will. The mind, the will, the thoughts, and the intentions are there in the "heart" of man.

Looking at the United Hearts of Jesus and Mary, I understood that the image symbolized a very intimate, honest, no-holds-barred connection and union between Them. But as I thought about the Immaculate Mary specifically, I began to understand the union more clearly.

First She was the Lord's Mother. She carried Him in Her womb, and as all mothers will tell you, that alone cultivates a special bond, or "union" between Them—even if only physically speaking. Jesus was flesh of Her flesh. His Sacred Heart grew and formed next to Her Heart for nine months. It was within Her Body that His Body took shape. It was nourishment from Her bloodstream, that His Blood began to form. (Those who feel they owe nothing to Mary should meditate on this for awhile...what Her fiat enabled to

71

take place. Those who believe She took no part in our redemption, should meditate on what Her body produced: the very instrument of our Redemption, the very Body and Blood of our salvation.) But even more than that, even more than their physical bond through DNA, Jesus and Mary share *spiritual* unity.

Think about it: it is sin that separates us from God, and it is the *rejection* of sin that draws us closer to Him. Mary was not only preserved from original sin, She remained sinless for Her entire life. The Immaculate Heart of Mary, therefore, is the epitome of Holy Love. She loved God above all else (perfectly), and Her neighbor as Herself (perfectly). Therefore, She is perfectly united to the Heart of God, which is Divine Love.

This unity between Jesus and Mary has been widely-criticized in recent years—by Protestants and Catholics alike...but it's not a new concept. Many popes, saints and doctors of the Church declared this an absolute truth. Over three hundred years ago, St. John Eudes spoke about the "mutual compenetration of the Hearts of Jesus and Mary". And Saint John Paul II coined the phrase "Alliance of the Two Hearts", when he referred to the union of Jesus and Mary in his Angelus address on September 15, 1985. Other well-known proponents are St. Bernard, St. Bonaventure, and St. Louis De Montfort, to name just a few.

Because of these references, and Monsignor Calkins' explanation of the 'heart', I was becoming more comfortable with the image of the United Hearts that was prominent throughout the ministry. But even more was being unveiled.

Upon opening the first book, I came across a message from Our Lady. "My daughter, it is time to make it known, that the United Hearts of Jesus and Mary are the New Kingdom, the New Jerusalem, **Holy and Divine Love**. I come to bring souls into this Kingdom." *(February 10, 1996)*

It dawned on me: *we* are called to live in Holy Love. Therefore, we are called to the same kind of union with God that Mary had. The United Hearts image, therefore, not only represents the union of Jesus and Mary, it represents Holy Love (human love) united to Divine Love (God's Love). It's an image of the human person united to God, through love. The image of the United Hearts, in a way, represents my own personal spiritual journey just as much as it does Mary's union with Her Son.

I thought back to my original trip to Holy Love Ministries (how I didn't know where I was headed), and the journey I was now on with this book (how I don't know where this is headed). I realized that this image of the United Hearts was the big, red X on the map of my new journey. This invitation from Mary wasn't just to some shrine in Ohio. It wasn't even an invitation to write a book. This was an invitation to a spiritual journey that leads to union with my Creator.

When we grow in Holy Love, we progress further down the path of salvation. We get closer and closer to the finish line—which is not our bodily death and entrance into afterlife, as I once had thought. The finish line is **union with God**—be it here on earth, or in the afterlife.

As Or Lady said, "when you are loving, My dear children, your hearts are already in Heaven." When we love, we are united to our Creator—to God, who is love. And *this* is Heaven. This is sanctification. This is what we were created for.

But let me be clear. I said "in union with" NOT "equal to." Unity with God and equal to God are two very different things. No one is equal to God. And unity simply means our desires become like God's desires and we live in unison with Him—professing what He professed, loving like He loved.

Clearly, the image of the United Hearts was *more* than just a representation of a Mother-Son relationship, as I had thought. Mary's Heart was an example of what souls of all faiths are called to be—in union with our Creator.

In essence, this image of the United Hearts is the destination on the map. It's the Light at the end of the tunnel. This is why we're here. What a revelation of purpose this is for souls! This image represents the end of the journey... but the more I read, the more I came to understand, it also represents the beginning.

"This is why He sends Me," Mary said, "so that I am able to lead you into union with [Jesus] through My own Heart." (February 9, 1997) At first I wondered what She meant by "Her own Heart". Did She mean simply that She leads us to Jesus through Holy Love (by teaching us how to love), or do we actually unite to Our Lady on this journey as well?

Jesus explained it further. "My Mother meets the souls who stand precariously on this threshold of conversion and salvation. She extends to them every grace they need to accept Her invitation to enter…Our United Hearts." (September 4, 2000)

I envisioned the image of the United Hearts as a large wall, a mystical threshold so to speak, painted entirely in the image of the destination. And there in the center, was the door—the Immaculate Heart of Mary.

Jesus said the key used for entry is the prayer to Mary Protectress of the Faith which was dictated to Maureen by Our Lady Herself on March 21 1997.

"Mary, Protectress of the Faith, shelter my faith in Your Immaculate Heart, Refuge of Holy Love. In the Refuge of Your Heart and united to the Sacred Heart of Jesus, Your Son, protect my faith from all evil. Amen."

"This simple prayer admits the soul into...the Immaculate Heart of Mary," Jesus said. "With Faith protected and Satan laid waste, the soul opens his heart to Holy Love." (October 16, 2000)

I envisioned the Heart of Mary to be like the foyer of a house—a room in itself, yes, but the entryway to so much more. With this small prayer, the door opens wide and the Blessed Virgin Mary swoops in. She covers us with Her mantle, hides us in Her Heart.

There, She shelters us from Satan's attacks—from pride, confusion, doubt. There, She sheds grace on our souls, which allows our hearts to open to a lifestyle of Holy Love. With open hearts, then, we take our first step forward... into Jesus.

This union with Our Lady and our Lord, was becoming clearer...But still, I wondered about all those people who don't believe the Virgin Mary has anything to do with the soul's salvation. There are *many* of them—even among Catholics. Is Mary still part of *their* journey?

Jesus explained it to Maureen, "...with or **without** knowing this, the soul who seeks his own salvation must gain entrance to...My Mother's Heart." (January 25, 2001) In other words, whether you know it or not, it happens. Mary invites us to walk with the Lord. She protects us, and sheds grace on our souls until we make the choice to move forward.

St. Louis De Montfort also spoke of this union with Mary, calling it, "a perfect path by which we go and unite ourselves to Jesus ...because Jesus, who has come to us most perfectly, took no other road for His great and admirable journey." [1]

Think about it. Jesus Himself crossed this same threshold, but coming from the other side. He stepped into earth, from the spiritual into the physical, and He did it by means of the Immaculate Heart of Mary.

He Himself entered physically into Her, into the beautiful foyer of Holy Love. There, He Himself took flesh, bones, even His Precious Blood. There He, too, was protected and nourished. He received everything He needed for His earthly journey, within Her. And after nine months, when He was made ready... the God of the universe entered the physical world.

If He who is the Creator of all things had such humility as to go through this doorway, who are we to say we do not need to do it? If we have agreed to "follow Him", how can we then reject His own passageway? Friends, like Him we must enter Her.

It is there that we, too, will receive everything necessary for the spiritual journey. There, within Mary, we will receive grace, strength, and protection. Then, when we

---

[1] True Devotion to Mary St. Louis DeMontfort Baronius Press, 2008, p. 99

are made ready in Her, we will step into union with Jesus, into the spiritual depths of the Holy Trinity.

I imagined this door to be a two-way, swinging door (like the kitchen door in a restaurant, where food servers go in and out). This is the door through which the Lord Himself came to us, and through which we must go back to Him.

But what is meant by "made ready"? How does the Blessed Virgin Mary "make us ready" for Jesus?

As Jesus said, "Once the soul gains admittance [to Mary's Heart]...his most glaring faults are brought to light..." (January 25, 2001)

I envisioned this foyer, this entryway of the Immaculate Heart, as just that   —immaculate, with stark white walls, white floor, white ceiling, full of light, adorned with white roses, white curtains and white chairs to rest your weary feet. No stain of sin can be found anywhere in Her.

Yet, here enters the human soul, after playing outside in worldly games. Upon entering such a place he can't help but realize his dirtiness. He becomes (in this immaculate foyer) keenly aware of his imperfections. He feels dirty and he is stunned by his filth. But... wait, there is hope.

"If (the soul) perseveres in grace," Jesus said, "these faults will be burned away..." (January 25, 2001)

If the soul remains in the foyer (instead of running from the realization of himself), he is cleansed. He is purified.

There is such an abundance of grace here, as we know from the revelation of the angel Gabriel when he said, "Hail Mary, full of grace!" (Luke 1:28) In Mary, the soul receives all the assistance he needs.

The Blessed Virgin Mary wraps Her mantle around the soul and Her Spouse, the Holy Spirit (who dwells in fullness here), comes with His Bride to greet souls at the door. He then, who is the Living Water of God, bathes them, fills them, and gives them Himself to drink. In this way, the soul is made ready.

As I read more and more of the messages in those books from Holy Love Ministries, it was all getting very complex, but at the same time, it was really quite simple. Once a soul comes to Mary, She not only protects him, but (through grace and the power of the Holy Spirit), She shows him those areas of his soul where he is severely lacking in love. After he is enlightened, if he continues on the path and lives more by way of Holy Love, then Mary sheds even more grace on his soul, and the "problem areas" are then overcome. This is done through the cooperation of the human will and grace.

This is not a new revelation, though. I found similar passages in a book called *The Way of Divine Love* written by visionary Sister Josepha Menedez. Sister Josepha, who over the course of several years in the early 1920s, recorded Jesus' words to her. Jesus said, "Love will purify you, will consume your defects, and the very strength of that pure and ardent love will lead you to sanctity..."[2] Clearly, the pure love He spoke of to Sr. Josepha was Holy Love, the Heart of the Immaculate Mary.

Pondering this, I thought about my own spiritual journey, specifically the time when I was away from the Faith. I was your typical fallen-away Catholic—unmoved by the Mass and irritated by the law.

I just couldn't understand it then. I mean, sure, my life had gone a bit 'askew', but I still considered myself a moral and decent person. I was certainly not in need of moral reform...as I thought the Church was implying.

But amidst all that angst, something was still quietly stirring my soul. Someone was still calling me from that two-way door. Sure, I remained outside for quite some time, sitting precariously on the fence. But She never stopped calling me. The Blessed Virgin Mary never (not for one, single instant) took Her eyes off me.

Who would have thought that years later I would be staring at an image of the United Hearts, totally committed to spreading Heaven's message. It's amazing, really. By the

---

[2] Way of Divine Love by Sr. Josepha Menedez, TAN Books & Publishers, Inc., 1972, p. 318

grace of God, this once bull-headed young woman actually became a Catholic in her heart. The funny thing is: at the time, I thought *conversion* was the destination. I thought *conversion* was the thing you eventually wound up at. I had no idea it was merely the swinging door that opened wide to a lifelong journey—a journey destined to arrive at unity with my Maker.

Huh. It's no wonder I was so lost then. I had no idea where I was headed.

CHAPTER 6

"The Map"

"My sister, long have I awaited this mission in the world, for it is a road map to salvation, holiness, and sanctity. What has not been laid bare before is now a road map beckoning all."
~Jesus (June 1, 2000)

In Our United Hearts are the secrets of life and death, of the cosmos, and time eternal."
~Blessed Mother (November 22, 1996)

"Understand that I am drawing you into a new dimension, a dimension of holiness and onto the path of righteousness. The path of light I lead you upon is eternal life."
~Blessed Mother (August 14, 1997)

"I come as always in praise of Jesus. I hope that you will realize through these visits, My dear children, that I am preparing you for the victory of Our United Hearts. This triumph can only come when Holy Love is triumphant in hearts. Dear children, please cooperate with My grace in bringing this victory into hearts."
~Blessed Mother (September 11, 1997)

Now that I finally understood the United Hearts a little better, I really combed through the books Don had given me. One book was especially eye -opening. It was called *Messages from St. Thomas Aquinas*. Lo and behold, after leafing through several pages, I discovered there was even *more* to the image of the United Hearts than I realized.

In fact, there was another illustration of the United Hearts, completely different from the first one. This image showed the *inside* of the Hearts—which were divided up into six compartments or "chambers", as they were called in the messages.

Salvation

Holy Love
Immaculate Heart of Mary

First Chamber

Holiness

Second Chamber

Perfection
in Virtue

Third Chamber

Sanctification
Conformity with
Divine Will
Fourth Chamber

Fifth
Chamber

Sixth
Chamber

© 2007 AGE

Union
with Divine Will
Fifth Chamber

Immersion
in the Divine Will
Sixth Chamber

In one message, Jesus said, "Our United Hearts represent a spiritual journey from the moment of conversion to Union with the Divine Will." *(August 24, 2000)*

"Ahhh. I get it." I thought. This illustration was the **roadmap**. Heaven revealed that the destination is union with God, and the entryway is the Immaculate Heart of Mary. If that wasn't enough, Our Lord was so kind as to actually draw us a map. And not just any map, a detailed, topographic map where we can see the many steep hills on the path of Holy Love—hills we *must* climb if we ever hope to ascend to the heights of Heaven.

It seemed a little weird at first: "chambers" of His Sacred Heart. But I came to see these chambers were simply different stages a soul passes through in the spiritual journey. Each stage was a new level of conversion that draws the soul nearer and nearer to God. At the end, the soul attains holy perfection and complete unity with its Creator.

It was like a curtain was being drawn in my mind revealing truths I had never known before. Lost in meditation, I began to imagine this spiritual journey as if it was a stroll through a garden paradise, where the soul is drawn deeper and deeper into the garden, toward its very center, where the fullness of God dwells in all His glory.

The soul walks through chamber after chamber. The first chamber as I have already said is the Immaculate Heart of Mary, the entryway, the garden foyer. Here, souls begin to see themselves as they are. Here, they either consent to the journey or head back out into the world. If they persevere and consent to the journey, the Blessed Mother leads them to the second chamber of the United Hearts. The second chamber is the Sacred Heart of Her Son, Jesus. Essentially, She opens for them a doorway to a beautiful garden paradise, the Heart of God.

THE SECOND CHAMBER

In the second chamber, the soul receives a new awareness of the spiritual life and must practice surrender. As Jesus said, "Little flaws in love come to light. After the soul drifts on the sea of calm when he is first admitted to the second chamber, he is able to see certain habits or attachments that hinder him from going deeper into Divine Love, My Heart. Waves of emotion toss him to and fro. At one moment the soul experiences dryness. The next moment he receives consolation." (October 17, 1999)

This is the beginning of the garden. Here there is a stream of Living Water. Little rays of the Light of the Son move across little, undeveloped plants (or unperfected virtues). Here, the soul begins to see little thorns on himself. He begins to notice little leaves, already brittle and brown, little stems already bent and broken. Here, he begins to see the soil of his faith in God—rocky and dry. But he also sees little buds of possibility.

In the second chamber, he receives the desire to work in the garden. Here, the soul is mesmerized by its beauty. He is excited to see the unfolding of all that has been planted here.

As Jesus said, " When a soul moves from Holy Love into Divine Love and the second chamber of My Heart, he receives a longing for a deepening of the virtues. The soul is developing a desire for holiness, but is uncertain as to how to attain it. It is during the soul's stay in this chamber that My grace comes to him, enticing him to a more devout life." (January 31, 2000)

In this level, it's as though the little rays of God's light, that dance across his heart, and captivate him. They fascinate him to such a degree that he yearns to follow them to their source. So he commits himself to the journey. He surrenders whatever it will cost him.

Jesus told Maureen on August 25, 2000, "As the soul surrenders more deeply to Holy Love, he passes into the second Chamber of My Sacred Heart, which is Divine Love. This is what takes place within the soul in this second Chamber which is holiness:

- The present moment is purified through a commitment to Divine Love.
- The soul surrenders his health, appearance and comforts.
- The soul begins to distinguish between his wants and his needs."

Here, the garden is new, small and fragile. But it is also here that Satan is on the prowl. Like a ferocious dog that threatens to trample the garden, he lurks and sneers.

"[This] is also the chamber where souls are most severely tested by Satan," Jesus said. "The soul needs to use heroic virtue in this chamber lest he slip into discouragement." (October 17, 1999)

THE THIRD CHAMBER

Next the soul moves into the third chamber. Here the rays of God's Light are much larger, more abound. The stream of Living Water is deeper, fuller, flowing more freely. Even the plants have grown a bit taller.

But, if any more progress is to be made, the soul must continue to work. Here, he begins the pruning. He must cut back all self love; he must uproot and pull out unhealthy attachments within his heart. In this way the virtues God has planted in his soul can begin to grow, flourish and bear fruit.

In the third chamber, the soul works tirelessly on landscaping. He perfects each and every virtue until it is pleasing to God.

Jesus said to Maureen, "As the soul attempts to polish the virtues in his heart and refine them in the eyes of God, he enters the third Chamber of My Heart. In this Chamber the soul finds himself tested over and over in every virtue, for it is the test that strengthens or weakens virtue according to the soul's response. This is the Chamber that fine-tunes holiness by testing the virtues as gold in the Flame of Divine Love. " (January 27, 2001)

"The soul can move as deeply into My Heart as he desires. The more he strips himself of self love, the deeper he grows in virtue and into the chambers of My Heart." (January 31, 2000)

"The [third chamber] brings noticeable change. The progress that the heart has made in the first two chambers comes to light. The flame of love in the heart of the soul spills out into the world around him. He is a martyr of love who strives to conform to the Divine Will of My Father." (April 7, 2000)

FOURTH CHAMBER

As the soul moves into the fourth chamber, he moves deeper into the garden. Here, there are no little rays, there is only Light, the fullness of light, everywhere. The stream of Living Water is a deep river that waters everything. Here, there are no more little plants, but rather a mighty oak (the Tree of Life) bearing a plentiful harvest of fruit. The roots are strong, long, and deep in the good soil of faith and trust. The branches are full and provide a welcomed hiddeness for the soul to commune with his Creator.

This is the goal of every soul. This is the center of the Heart of God, the center of the garden and His Kingdom. This, my friends, is Heaven.

"The souls, and few there are, whom I select from the Third Chamber as My saints and martyrs of love come into the Fourth and most intimate Chamber. " Jesus said. (October 20, 1999)

He continued, "Within the fourth chamber of My Heart, united to the Divine Will of My Father, are all the angels of Heaven. Yes! Myriads upon myriads of angels! Moreover, within this chamber is every soul in Heaven. Think of it! Every saint is here in My Heart, in the Will of the Father. This is why I tell you, you can obtain Heaven on earth when you live in My Father's Divine Will. All the other chambers are but preparation for this fourth chamber. In the other chambers, the souls are trying to conform to the Divine Will through conviction of conscience and elimination of self love. But the victory and sanctification of every soul is this

cherished fourth chamber of My Most Sacred Heart."
(February 21, 2000)

"[The soul who arrives in the fourth chamber] desires to be in this chamber more than anything else. Through his desire to be united with Me, he has surrendered all his own wants—that is to say, his own will. Such a soul knows full well his littleness before God. He does not seek laud or recognition for any good deed, for he knows all goodness flows from God. In his humility he desires hiddenness. He longs for littleness in the eyes of the world. Thus, the soul is steeped in humility and meekness."

"When the soul experiences any trial, he returns it immediately to Me. Therefore, we share each cross together. The soul in the fourth chamber of My Heart does not know fear. He is always at peace, even in the midst of the greatest trial. In every present moment such a soul sees God's Holy and Divine Will. The fourth chamber of My Heart is the ultimate goal of every soul, though few attain it." (December 18, 1999)

THE FIFTH CHAMBER

But even this is still not the ***highest*** Heaven. Souls can discover still more. In fact, it is possible for souls to enter a fifth chamber, an "inner sanctum" within the fourth chamber as Jesus called it on April 17, 2000.

As the soul explores the glory of the fourth chamber, he discovers another area... even more beautiful. The difference is this: in the 4th chamber the soul still makes an effort in conforming his will to God's will. He still weeds the garden of his heart, prunes what God has planted, and draws water from the stream.

But, in the fifth chamber, he no longer needs to make this effort. In this area of the garden, virtue and love simply exist. The soul bears fruit. The soil of his faith does not need to be watered, either. It is wet already. It is as if this area of the garden was planted right in the stream. The drops of the stream's water mingle with the granules of soil in perfect harmony. In the fourth chamber there are still two entities: water and soil. In the fifth chamber, however, the water of the Holy Spirit *penetrates* the soil of the soul. The human will is united to the Divine Will and they now exist as one—wet soil.

Jesus explained to Maureen, " I have come to help you understand the depth of the fourth chamber of My Heart. Within this chamber is an inner sanctum - some may term it a fifth chamber—which few souls have entered from the beginning of time. The hearts that enter this sanctuary never think of self. Their will is completely annihilated and the Divine Will of My Father reigns supreme. The Will of God is the height and breadth, indeed the substance of this sanctuary of peace, as is every soul thus admitted." (April 17, 2000)

" [The fifth chamber] is the smallest, most elite chamber comprised of the most humble and loving souls. The souls that dwell herein are part of My Heart. They no longer are part of the world, but I am in them. They only exist to accomplish the Father's Will. Such as these give to Me every present moment. They disappear only to be replaced by the Will of My Father." (April 12, 2000)

"In this [fifth] chamber the soul exists and is completely absorbed in the Divine Will. The person no longer lives, but the Will of God lives through him. He accepts everything as from the Hand of My Father, knowing everything is a grace and all things turn to the good of his salvation. Every virtue has been fine-tuned. The kingdom of the Divine Will reigns within his heart. This kingdom is the triumph of Our United Hearts."

SIXTH CHAMBER

Yes, you read that right. The fifth chamber is still not the highest Heaven. There is still one more chamber. There is a sixth chamber, which is the Heart of the Eternal Father.

Here, the human will is not *united* to the Divine Will, it is **immersed** in it. Here the granules of the soil do not mix with the drops of the stream's water, they dissolve into the ocean of it and melt away completely.

Here, the soul does not just grow in the light, it glows with the light. The light and the bloom merge and become a new creation...radiant, full of the glory of God, resplendent and glorified, much like the body of Jesus at the Transfiguration on Mt. Tabor.

" He was transfigured before them; his face shone like the sun and his clothes became white as light." (Matthew 17:2)

Here, the soul is made in the true Image of Christ. Here, the soul reaches and is immersed in the very source of the Light that he was drawn to at the beginning of the journey — that is, the Eternal Father.

As St. Margaret Mary Alacoque explained to Maureen, "The Sixth Chamber is the embrace of the Heart of God which is the Divine Will. The soul feels the embrace of the Father's Heart increase as his soul is drawn deeper into the Chambers of the United Hearts. This being so, please see that as the soul is drawn into the First Chamber, he feels the Father's embrace begin. Each subsequent Chamber allows the soul to feel the Father's embrace increase. The Eternal

Father tries to draw each soul into the highest Heaven."
(April 2, 2000)

St. Thomas Aquinas then told Maureen, "In the Sixth Chamber the human will is immersed in the Divine Will so that they are, so to speak, mixed together. No longer can one be distinguished from the other. As St. Paul said, 'It is no longer I who live, but Christ who lives through me.' The two wills—the Divine Will and the free will—are blended together, one immersed in the other, to become one." (April 2, 2000)

I began to look through the pile of books from Don on my kitchen table, to see if there was another compilation of messages that might enlighten me further. But there in the midst of them I found a completely different book. It was the *Introduction to the Devout Life* by St. Francis De Sales—the one that Fr. David had given me. I hadn't had time to look at it as of yet, but there it was on my kitchen table, displaced in a pile of books from Holy Love Ministries.

I picked it up and opened to the contents. "It's quite a *lengthy* listing for being merely an introduction," I thought. It was five parts long, with twenty or so chapters in each part. Each part seemed to describe a phase of the spiritual life. Then it dawned on me. It was *five* parts long.

"Could it be?" I wondered.

I looked through the chapters and was shocked to find that each of the five parts of St. Francis' book was similar to each of the first five Chambers of the United Hearts.

For example, in the first part he talked about purifying the soul, just as Mary helps us do in the First Chamber. In the second part, he talked about prayer, meditation and Mass, similar to the Second Chamber where the soul works on holiness and the sacraments. In the third part of his book, St. Francis discusses the how the soul can perfect the virtues, which is identical to the Third Chamber.

In the fourth part, he talks about disregarding the criticisms of this world and wanting what God wants. Or as the Fourth Chamber explains: seeking conformity with God's Will. In the fifth part, St. Francis discusses the excellence of the soul...which I imagine only comes from being in Union with God (being in the Fifth Chamber).

Later, I discovered another book called 'Interior Castle' by St. Teresa of Avila... another doctor of the Church.

In it she says, "I began to think of the soul as if it were a castle made of a single diamond or of very clear crystal, in which there are many rooms, just as in Heaven there are many mansions."

The entire book describes the soul's journey through these different "rooms" in the castle... how the soul progresses from an imperfect, sinful creature to the "Bride of the Spiritual Marriage," as she calls it.

This book is also comparable to the chambers that Jesus and Mary have been explaining to Maureen. St. Teresa described _seven_ rooms, however. But, as I looked closer, I realized she included the "outer realm" as a room. The outer room is where she says the soul is still "very much in love with the venomous creatures outside the castle...[where] all is cold and dim." This does not appear to be a room _within_ the castle. Therefore, she describes six rooms within the castle...just like the six chambers.

She describes six rooms, similar to the chambers. She describes the room of prayer and self-knowledge, then virtue, then conformity to God's Will, then union, and finally the merge or "Spiritual Marriage".

Now, I am not a theologian. But two Catholic Saints (doctors of the Church) have already clearly spoken about this spiritual journey.

This set my heart at ease for two reasons. One, as Fr. David said, "You can judge apparitions by comparing the messages with other, approved texts. There should be nothing new revealed in apparitions. Apparitions merely re-state things in new ways for evolving cultures."

I felt secure with the revelation of the United Hearts because many others had spoken of this union before...but

Chambers? Earlier, as I pondered them, I recalled Father David's words in the back of my mind, and even though the journey made so much sense to me, I had that nagging suspicion whether I should believe in a revelation so new as to describe "compartments" of our Lord's Sacred Heart.

But now I understood it was not new at all. St. Francis De Sales discussed this journey in lengthy detail almost 400 years ago when he published his now Church-approved and highly recommended *Introduction* on spirituality. And St. Teresa also discussed it in the 1500s in another Catholic Classic.

I also realized the gravity of what this revelation meant for souls!! The human story began in a garden, the garden of Eden. Yes, Adam and Eve were kicked out of the garden because of disobedience, but that did not change God's plan. God's original plan was to live with His children for all eternity in the garden of paradise, in His kingdom... and He will, still, even after Adam and Eve's fall into sin. This is how!

Nailed to the tree of Life Jesus re-opened the "garden" for souls. On Pentecost, the Holy Spirit brought the garden into the untouchable, spiritual dimension.

Here, the soul journeys deeper and deeper through the Hearts of Mary and Jesus, where at last he finds God the Father—where at last he finds the paradise lost.

But don't take my word for it. The Scriptures are full of instances that point to this internal, spiritual journey...

Romans 12:1 says "let God transform you inwardly."

In John 4:14, Jesus says, "the water I shall give will turn into a spring inside him, welling up to eternal life."

Philipians 2:13 says "God is at work in you."

1 Thess. 5:23 says "May the God of peace sanctify you wholly."

Ephesians 4:22 says we must "put away our old way of life... and be renewed by a spiritual revolution..."

In John 14:23 Jesus said, "Anyone who loves me, will obey my teaching. My Father will love them, and we will come to them and make our home with them."

Another thing I realized: I had accepted the Blessed Mother's invitation to write this book and take this journey, but it wasn't until leafing through messages on the chambers that I realized everything it would require of me. And I don't mean in terms of hours of work. I mean in terms of the hills I must climb in order to get to the heights of Heaven. It would require that I practice virtue and learn to love better...which is quite a bit harder than juggling a work schedule and writing a few chapters.

In that moment, I realized the seriousness of the road I was about to embark on. This was a transforming journey of the human heart. Seeing all the work that had to be done along the way… well, it terrified me. My heart was one of the weaker ones.

My heart was willing but—like an out of shape runner at the start of a marathon—it was hardly ready. It was excited, but it was scared. I was usually very good at setting goals, working hard and accomplishing things. And if this were a regular foot race, I'd probably do ok with some training.

But this was different. This was a journey of the heart. This meant being open to the grace of correction, to humility and admitting my faults and failures. This meant putting God first no matter what anyone else thinks, and loving my neighbors (all neighbors) as myself. This was unlike anything else I'd ever set out to do before.

But, by the grace of God I had been given the map. I had no more excuses for not taking this journey seriously. I closed the books from Don and just sat at my kitchen table. Everything seemed different. Everything. Heaven had reached down, touched my little world, and shook things up.

It was like I had been living as a wanderer or a drifter my whole life, and now suddenly I was a pilgrim. I had a vision, a purpose, a destination. The once mundane day-to-day became a very sacred journey.

Perhaps this is what Don meant when he said, "Sometimes people receive a different kind of grace at the shrine." I had received an awakening in my soul... like my heart had just awoken from a lifelong nap to reality. It was just like the hand-written message Maureen showed me. Jesus had truly embraced my heart.

CHAPTER 7

"The Resistance"

"Today, My children are engaged in heart-to-heart, hand-to-hand combat with My adversary. Evil influence has invaded every nation and all phases of life. Satan is in music, literature, television and movies; modern medicine, even certain modes of dress. He has infiltrated governments and political actions - yes, even the Church itself. To deny this is to be his cohort."
~Blessed Mother (June 27, 2003)

"Dear children, with docility, understand what I am here to tell you... A wound needs to be exposed to the air to finally heal. [She smiles and motions towards the scratch on Maureen's arm.] So it is with the bride. Her spouse allows her wounds to come into the light so that a healing can take place from the inside out. Some, in astonishment, say, `Look at the depth of the woundedness.' Remember, My Son is the Divine Physician, and can heal all wounds. He even has sent His own Mother to you as `Protectress of the Faith', a title which is healing in itself. So much does He love you and desire that you have only the truth, for He is the Truth.
~Blessed Mother (September 15, 2006)

"...the messages lay bare Satan—his snares and his tactics. Do not be surprised at the inroads Satan has made where he is exposed...This could not remain under the cover of darkness any longer. While it is bringing down those in high places, even within the Church, it is necessary in order that the festering sore be healed."
~Blessed Mother (April 5, 2002)

The weeks flew by, as they typically do in summer, and before I knew it I was heading off to Ohio for my first interview with Maureen. It was a gray and rainy morning, but two close friends from my bible study, Lori and Tina, agreed to come with me in spite of it. Neither of them had been to the Shrine yet and so they were excited about the journey. While in the car, however, Tina told us of a disheartening experience she had earlier in the week.

A woman from our parish warned her not to go to Maranatha Spring. "She told me it was condemned by the Church," Tina said, still a little upset about it.

I wasn't sure how to respond. At the time, I knew nothing about Maranatha Spring being "condemned," and couldn't imagine why in the world it would be. The messages were so beautiful and had already produced so much fruit in my life that I couldn't understand how anyone could really feel this way.

At the time, I just assumed the condemnation was a rumor, typical in our small town, and I got very upset seeing how it had disturbed Tina. She had been looking forward to this trip and I couldn't understand why anyone would want to ruin it for her, especially given her situation.

Tina had been struggling with cancer for quite some time...though, like a trooper, she was beating all odds. Her tumor was not growing larger, but her spirits were. She accepted her situation with confidence that the Lord was working in her life.

"Someday Jesus is going to heal me," She said. **

I smiled, recalling the Lord's words in Scripture, "O woman, great is thy faith: be it done unto thee...as thou wilt." (Mt. 15:28)

When we arrived at Maranatha, I went to meet with Maureen, and left Tina and Lori to their pilgrimage. A priest named Fr. Mike, Maureen's Spiritual Advisor, joined us and we sat down for a comfortable conversation. The interview questions that I conjured up were rather vague—as was my knowledge about the how this place came to be.

"I guess we could start with some background information," I said. "When and how did the Blessed Mother first appear to you?"

"Well, I was at Adoration at a neighborhood Church," Maureen said. "And Our Lady was suddenly just standing to the side of the Monstrance—She never puts her back to Jesus or the Blessed Sacrament. She had a large beaded rosary in her hands and I thought, 'Am I the only one seeing her?' People were getting up and leaving, or coming in and not paying any attention. All of a sudden the fifty Hail Mary beads turned into the shapes of the fifty states. Then she left. I didn't know why she was there, but I thought, 'maybe she wants me to pray for the country.'"

"What did you do after that?" I pried. "Did you tell anyone?"

"There was one man who ran Adoration and I told him what I saw, but I didn't want other people to know. Then later, I started getting messages—first from Jesus, then from Mary. But I didn't tell anybody about them.

"At the time though, I joined a charismatic prayer group. At one of the meetings, a man got up and said, 'There's someone here who is getting messages and not speaking them.'

"I thought, 'oh no!' Then he said, 'we'll turn off the air conditioner in case you have a quiet voice, so everybody can hear you.' Well, they knew instantly that it was me because I was the only one who was being quiet at these meetings. I went out of there crying, and I quit the prayer group.

"Then I went back to see the first man, who ran Adoration. He said for me to just give him the messages and he would get up and read them. No one would have to know I was getting them. I said, okay, and that's when I first started to write them down."

"Were you ever asked to go to see the Bishop or anyone else in the Church?" I asked. (This was a typical request of Our Lady in other apparitions.)

"Yes." She said. "Our Lady gave me the title 'Mary

Protectress of the Faith' in 1986 with a small prayer. She wanted the title to have Church approval so that it could spread throughout the country...So I took it to a priest who seemed very devoted to the Blessed Mother and he sent it to Bishop Pilla's office, along with a lot of other messages.

"Then Our Lady came to me and said, 'Jesus wants you to know that not everyone will agree and believe in these messages.' I thought, 'Well, why wouldn't they? What's the problem with the messages?' So, I sort of ignored it. But things slowly started to cave in."

"What caved in?" I asked.

Fr. Mike spoke up. "Well first, Maureen was supposed to remain anonymous. And the Diocese exposed her identity."

"Then, they wouldn't approve the title," Maureen added. "They said that there were already too many devotions to the Blessed Mother and the saints, and that She didn't need that title."

"They also used the excuse that the Holy Spirit is already called the Guardian of the Faith," Fr. Mike said. "And that is true. But people sometimes lose sight of the fact, especially in Catholic circles, that the Blessed Mother is espoused to the Holy Spirit."

"So we went to someone in the Marionite order," Maureen said. "His name was Core Bishop Webby, from New

York. We wanted to see if he could give us a NIHL OBSTAT, a Church approval. And he did. But later, he wrote a letter saying he had to withdraw it...Well, he *could* approve it. He just chose not to because other Church officials were complaining.

"It was so hard," Maureen continued. "I didn't know there was all this political stuff in the Church or that they would have reason to object to anything. I just knew Our Lady said people were going to need Her protection in the latter days. And now we see why."

I personally didn't really understand. But Maureen continued talking, so I decided to let it go...for now.

"In 1990, Blessed Mother asked us to form this prayer group called Project Mercy," she said. "The idea was to go into churches and form groups that would meet after Mass to pray against abortion. I went to see an Auxiliary Bishop who said, 'You really can't go into churches and pray against abortion because our insurance doesn't cover it.'

"I think the real problem was they didn't want Blessed Mother appearing in their Churches. They knew if I prayed, then the Blessed Mother would come. Then that would look like their Church approved Her coming. So, we had this group of people who wanted to pray the rosary, and wanted to meet weekly, but we had no place to pray."

Hearing her tell this story was amazing. They went

through so much, just to be able to pray the rosary. They tried church after church, but no one would let them pray in their building. I felt so sheltered, not knowing all this was taking place in a Catholic diocese only two hours away from me.

"We couldn't even pray in the Byzantine and Orthodox Churches...so we decided to pray in the woods," Maureen said. "And people kept coming—with their walkers! People had wheelchairs on their backs, traipsing through the mud. It was crazy!"

Fr. Mike laughed, "It really was. Don was copying messages from the tape recorder, using tree trunks!"

"That's when Blessed Mother told us to go look for property in South Lorain County which is where we're at now," Maureen continued. "I begged Her, 'Please Blessed Mother, let us pray in another diocese!'

"But She said no. She said 'Like it or not, we're praying here. And we're praying for them.' The whole thing was very scary to me. I remember thinking, 'How did I get into this?' I just wanted to pray the rosary."

"After you purchased this property did things get better?" I asked. "You now have rosary services here almost daily...does the Diocese still try and stop you?"

"Well," she began. "In 1996, we were called down to meet with the Chancellor here in Cleveland, and a few others.

Blessed Mother told me to get a Canon lawyer to go with us. So Fr. Kenney, my Spiritual Advisor at the time, called all over the country."

After much searching Fr. Kenney found a canon lawyer willing to help. They sent him the messages, and after reading them thoroughly, told Fr. Kenney, Maureen and Don that there was nothing wrong with them. He then accompanied them to the meeting with the Chancellor at the Cleveland diocese.

"[Our lawyer] said that this was an ecumenical ministry, and that the diocese couldn't control it. And that is true. We *are* ecumenical because the Blessed Mother says the messages are for all people of all Faiths.

"I guess I should have been happy with the way things played out," Maureen said. "But I was devastated. Even though Blessed Mother told me that Jesus wanted me to know not everyone would believe in it, I certainly thought the Bishop and the Chancellor would. I never thought we'd have to go so far as to take a lawyer with us."

Fr. Mike added, "This is what Maureen has had to struggle with throughout this process. When you're a faithful Catholic, your desire is to be obedient to the hierarchy of the Church. And throughout this whole process she has felt like she's *not* being obedient. But the Blessed Mother and Jesus keep coming to her, encouraging her."

"Yes," she agreed. "Throughout it all, they have kept coming and talking to me, reassuring me that there was a mission here someplace. And now, through this mission, people are being encouraged to look for the truth. Most people assume that if the Bishop says something, you have to be obedient, that it doesn't matter if what he says is right or wrong."

Fr. Mike spoke up. "But he is not living the faith we are supposed to live...'"

"How so?" I asked. There was a pause, a very long pause.

"You must've heard what happened in the Boston Diocese?" Fr. Mike asked, referring to the pedophilia scandal in which numerous priests were investigated. "Well, it was three times worse here in Cleveland, under Bishop Pilla. Nearly 500 people, who were closely tied to the Church, were investigated. 145 of them were priests. Plus, there was a lot of financial scandal...not to mention, FutureChurch."

"What's FutureChurch?" I asked.

Fr. Mike adjusted himself more comfortably in his seat. "Well," he said. "It's an organization... which basically says there should be a more democratic process to the Catholic Church...that priests should be *elected* to their position, etc. But FutureChurch takes it one step further, claiming there should be women who are ordained to the priesthood, and that it's okay for homosexuals to be ordained, as well. It's basically total dissonance against Rome."

"The biggest thing though," Maureen added. "Is that they say the conscience holds priority over anything that the Church teaches. Basically, they think that if you feel it is okay to do something, then it's okay. It doesn't matter whether your conscience is formed in righteousness or not." She looked at Fr. Mike. "Maybe I should get Don."

He nodded, "yeah, bring Don in."

Don was in the other room doing paperwork, but came in shortly with a stack of newspaper clippings, photos and magazine articles. "I thought this was supposed to be on Maranatha Spring and Shrine," he said. "Not the diocese." He was looking around the room. No one said anything. And I realized they were just as unsure how to proceed with this information as I was.

"I think it's all related, isn't it?" Maureen said.

"I guess." Don answered. "Anyway, you just can't imagine it, Stace," laying some papers in front of me. As a retired cop, he had certainly done his homework. "FutureChurch calls itself Catholic," he said.

"But they're turning the Catholic Faith upside down," Father noted. "They honor Mary Magdalene, but they put her in witch-like attire."

110

"They also have a statue of the Blessed Mother," Maureen said. "...but it's a naked statue of her."

"No way," I thought. I was in shock, utter shock. A naked statue of the Blessed Mother? This can't be for real. It just can't be.

"But what does FutureChurch have to do with the Diocese, if it's total dissonance to Rome?" I asked. "Isn't it then a separate entity, a completely different Church, if it's not associated with the Vatican?"

Don laid a newspaper clipping in front of me with a photo of the naked statue of the Blessed Mother. The headline read "Chancellor Defends Nude Statue".

"The diocese is defending it?" I asked.

"Not just defending it," Don said, laying another newspaper article in front of me. "They're funding it."

"No way," I thought again. *"This can't possibly be true."* But there in front of me was a large stack of resources that claimed it absolutely ***was*** true—highly respected sources such as the *Plain Dealer*, Cleveland's largest newspaper.

Allegedly Joe Smith, the Chief Financial Officer for the Diocese, was under investigation for the disappearance of several million dollars of the Church's money.[3] As it turned out, some of it went to FutureChurch. Not to mention,

---

[3] *Crimes Against Catholics* by Bill Frogameni, SCENE, September 6-12, 2006

FutureChurch has been operating, for free, out of Catholic Churches—St. Mark's in Lakewood, for example.

I couldn't believe my eyes. This wasn't just any missing money...this was money that the elderly and hard working families put into the collection baskets every Sunday—money given with the intent of helping the poor and funding the Lord's Church. Instead, it was used to help a schismatic group fund the spread of heresy and witchcraft?

I wondered though, how this could be the fault of Bishop Pilla. Joe Smith was a lay employee, and as criminal as he was, could have steered the money secretly.

But several reports claimed Bishop Pilla knew all about it.

Joe Smith worked directly under financial and legal secretary Fr. John Wright, who created a special fund that paid Smith $270,000 in unreported income, in addition to his regular salary. And Santiago Feliciano, the diocese's former general counsel, who spent 22 years working for the Church, said Bishop Pilla was the only person Fr. Wright answered to. He also said the Bishop was a "micromanager, especially with money...No way would this amount of money have been transferred without [Pilla's] say-so." [4]

---

[4] *Crimes Against Catholics* by Bill Frogameni, SCENE, September 6-12, 2006

As hard as it was to swallow, it all started making sense—why the Virgin Mary came to the Cleveland Diocese as *Protectress of the Faith*, why She was asking Maureen to pray for the very people who were turning her away...even why She encouraged her to continue the mission, in spite of the Diocese's attempts to thwart their plans.

It also made sense now, why the Diocese didn't want Maureen to pray in their Churches. They didn't want the *Virgin Mary* in their Churches. Probably because they knew She would likely have something to say about their statue of Her.

"At one point Blessed Mother told me there are two Churches now," Maureen said. "One is run by Satan and one is run by Her Son."

"That's just it," Don added. "This isn't just happening in Cleveland. FutureChurch, pedophilia...this filth is everywhere. Cleveland just happens to be a hotbed for it."

"Bishop Pilla could have really done some good across the country as President of the Council of Catholic Bishops," Maureen said, "if he would have promoted the title, "Mary, Protectress of the Faith". But Blessed Mother said he has made himself the enemy of this mission." Maureen took a deep sigh. "I'm praying for him every day, still."

"It's hard for us," Don said. "We grew up in the old

days. We remember when Catholics looked up to the priests and the nuns; they were next to God. We certainly never wanted to be put in a position where we had to go against one. But Jesus said there is a difference between *blind* obedience and obedience to Him—especially in these horrible times."

"And they are horrible," Father agreed. "Jesus said in a recent message that today's world is a thousand times worse than Sodom and Gomorrah was. I do believe we're in the latter days now."

I nodded, but not really sure what to make of it all.

"But," Father Mike added, "Bishop Pilla resigned. And there is a new Bishop here in Cleveland, who was just installed in May (2006)—Bishop Lennon is his name. He actually came from the Boston area. He's made some significant changes already. He's banned any meetings of FutureChurch in any of the Churches in the diocese, and he's going around making unannounced visits to parishes. So maybe we're seeing the start of a turnaround."

The problem however, was that the already established FutureChurch was now capable of building their own Churches and could survive apart from Catholic buildings, thanks to the initial help from the Diocese.

With that, we wrapped up our first interview and agreed to continue the discussion in a couple weeks.

Maureen hugged me and thanked me for my help. Don gave me copies of several newspaper clippings and magazine articles and walked me to the door. It was raining still, but warm. I called Lori on my cell phone to see where they were at and to let them know I was finished. They had just walked into the gift shop.

"Do you want us to drive over and pick you up, since it's raining?" she asked.

"No, that's okay." I told her. I needed a few minutes to be alone and clear my head. "I'll walk over there."

"If you're sure..." she said.

"I'm sure."

"If we're not still in the book store when you get here, then we'll be in the prayer center."

"I'll find you," I assured her.

"Okay..." she said. "Hey...are you alright?"

"Yep. I'm fine...just looking forward to a peaceful walk."

"Okay, we'll see you soon."

"See you soon." I said, and we hung up.

I put my tape recorder and everything from the interview safely in my backpack, strapped it on my back and began walking. Church disapproval, schisms and scandals...what was I getting myself into?

I thought of the woman from our parish who

warned Tina not to go to Maranatha Spring & Shrine. Obviously she knew more than I did at this point, and I felt a bit naïve...and disobedient. As I walked, however, I breathed in an air of peace, and I knew in my heart that Maranatha Spring was for real. I knew in my soul that Heaven was trying to reach out to mankind through this site and these messages. I knew the awakening I had in my own heart and soul was real.

I stopped at the Lake of Tears. Not a soul was around. I sat down on a bench, and moaned out loud. *"What am I doing?"* I thought. *"I can't do this...I can't get involved in something this big!"*

I looked up at the vast, gray sky raining down on me, and the enormity of it was humbling. It seemed so huge, so immeasurable, so uncontrollable. I felt like a spec of sand, and was almost cowering at the immensity of it. Then, in my heart I heard the words, "You're right. *You* can't do this."

Sitting on that bench, under an endless sky, I became profoundly aware of my nothingness—and the Lord's infinite power. And I realized it was true. I could *not* do *anything*, by myself. I was but an instrument—a pen without ink, at very best—completely useless.

But it is God Almighty, eternal commander of the endless sky, who (for reasons beyond my comprehension) wishes to use me. So what have I to fear? If the All-Powerful picks me up and commands, "write what I have said" would He not fill me with spiritual ink, His Holy Spirit... the same way He fills the clouds with rain?

The rain was soaking my hair, which was now dripping down my face, and I began to think. We don't always like the rain. We prefer sunshine. But God allows us to experience it, to see it, and feel the dampening effects it has on our bodies, because it is necessary in bringing life to our planet.

I thought of the scandals within the Church. I might not like it. I might prefer a sunny-kind of faith. But God has allowed us to experience this apostasy. He wants us to see it and feel the dampening effects it has on our spirits, because the *Truth* is necessary in bringing life to our souls.

Truly, there is a fingerprint of Satan on the heart of our Church today. The areas of schism and heresy are paths that the devil carved out to lure souls away from God. And now, through the messages given to Maureen, Our Lady and Jesus want to unveil these paths for what they truly are— dead end roads. I stood up, closed my eyes and put my face to the sky. I breathed in, felt strength, and continued my walk.

"Yes, this story is bigger than me," I thought. *"But not bigger than my God."*

The doubt and anxiety were gone, completely gone.

And I knew firsthand what my mother meant when she said, "Mary took it from me, back at that Lake."

I found Tina and Lori in the gift shop. It was 3:00 and so we went over to the prayer center where they were praying the Chaplet of Divine Mercy. Afterwards, we packed up and headed for home.

It was a little quiet in the car, at first. We talked about some of the pictures in the prayer center. I commented on how many people capture circles in their photographs—a sign of Our Lady's presence, which She noted in a message to Maureen. (Nov. 8, 1996)

Then Lori spoke up. "Something weird happened when we were at the Lake of Tears," she said. "I didn't understand it then, until just now."

"What was it?" Tina asked.

"Well, I bent down to rinse off my hands in the water. Tina, when I stood up and looked across the Lake at you..." She paused. "Well, there was a big circle of light floating behind you. I blinked my eyes and rubbed them. I thought maybe I was seeing sun spots... but it was dark and rainy. The circle followed you around the Lake and then it disappeared. It floated into your back."

I looked over at Tina in the front passenger seat. She was staring straight ahead and smiling, calmly. She didn't say a word but her face assured me that somehow, she felt what

Lori saw. I guess my mother and I aren't the only ones who have been deeply touched at that Lake of Tears.

** Update:

It was about two years after this trip, and I was pulling into the parking lot of a local coffee shop. I had my briefcase and my lap top, ready to work on this book.

As I parked the car, my cell phone rang. It was Tina, calling me to ask (as she often did) about this book.

"Is it done yet? I can't wait to read it!" she said.

At the time, it was not finished. I think she knew that. I think her asking was an excuse, a reason to call and talk (as if she needed one).

I shut the car off and sat in the driver's seat. The sun was shining. The birds were chirping. The Lord's blessings were blowing lightly in the spring breeze. And Tina and I chatted.

Her tumor was now much larger than before, and at her last appointment, her doctor was grim. He spoke frankly to her and did not have much confidence in a recovery.

Tina spoke to me about what she had always thought (that Jesus would heal her), and what now seemed to be playing out. And for the first time since her diagnosis, Tina wondered if perhaps she was dying.

Despite this, however, there was still joy in her spirit.

She was bursting with gratitude for the litany of things the Lord had recently done in her life. Even though she faced death, she still had trust in her God, and every syllable she uttered seemed to praise His Divine plan.

I sat in my car, marveling at what I was blessed to be witness to. My dear friend, Tina, had arrived at a very holy place in her journey. She had arrived at complete conformity with God's will (the fourth chamber). The most beautiful part was that she didn't even realize it.

I recalled a message from Jesus: "The soul in the fourth chamber of My Heart does not know fear. [She] is always at peace, even in the midst of the greatest trial. In every present moment such a soul sees God's Holy and Divine Will. The fourth chamber of My Heart is the ultimate goal of every soul, though few attain it." (December 18, 1999)

Tina and I talked for quite some time, about the mysterious plan of God and the acceptance of His Will. Before we hung up the phone, we each told the other, "I love you". That was the last time I spoke with Tina. She passed away a few days later... though not before telling the priest who was present, "Father, Jesus healed me!"

Truly He had. Tina was sanctified, healed of self-will, conformed entirely to the image and likeness of Christ who prayed, "Father, let not My will, but Yours be done." She had, as Scripture says, crucified the flesh.

After her death, I thought a lot about the circle of light that Lori saw over Tina on our trip. And I knew Our Lady had much to do with her "healing". Once again, it was just as Don said the first time he and I met at the Spring, "Sometimes people receive a different kind of grace [at this Shrine]—the kind that gives a person strength to endure, or enlightenment to understand their situation."

To this day I am so grateful for Our Lady, for giving my dear friend this grace, the grace to move through the United Hearts, and to pass peacefully and joyfully from this world to eternity.

CHAPTER 8

"The Strategy"

"You must be strong during these last battles. If you are judged and misunderstood, remember so too was I."
~Jesus (April 6, 1999)

"Today I will teach you about holy Humility, as humility and love go hand in hand. A soul cannot progress along the path to the Kingdom of Divine Love outside of either of these two. The humble soul has died to his self-will. He has surrendered all to Me, and I to the Father."
~Jesus (January 13, 1999)

"Without your surrender, I cannot achieve in you My goal and your salvation...Self-surrender is My call for you to give up your own will...Your self-surrender is what moves your feet up the staircase of holiness... I cannot resist such a one."
~Jesus (May 21, 1999)

"I do not promise this path will be trouble-free. Satan, the flesh, and the world oppose it. It is not popular to those who desire immediate gratification. But surrender is sweet and palatable to those who love Me. To these it is love itself, peace and joy."
~Jesus (May 29, 1999)

I returned home from our first interview in a very solemn state, confounded by the seriousness of what had been brought to my attention. The Roman Catholic Faith that I had come to love so deeply was under attack...as were its members. What was even worse: Our Lady came to Ohio to warn the Church and protect it from these attacks, but few will listen or take heed. When I returned home, I discovered first hand just how few.

Someone very close to me—who is also Catholic— did not think I should get involved. "You can't just go against Bishops! It's not right," they said.

Another close friend from my parish expressed concern regarding the term United Hearts. "Mary has nothing to do with my salvation," she said, "Nothing. And it's dangerous to assume She is in anyway 'united' to God."

In another instance, I was telling a few friends in my bible study about the messages. One woman spoke up and cautioned the group. "You know, this isn't approved by the Church." She said. Then she looked at me. "I'm sorry. I just don't want everyone going home with their heads in the clouds."

Several others approached me with similar opinions, but what hurt most was the fact that they came from my friends—and my friends were respectable people. They were good Catholics, who loved the Lord and loved the

Church...and had been faithful to both for a lot longer than I had been. They weren't trying to be heretical or dissenting. They were just concerned. I began to feel like a naïve and confused little girl in the eyes of my peers and my friends.

The most crushing concerns, however, came directly after the July 06 issue of the Gist hit newsstands. In the Letters to the Editor section, we printed two letters from readers who expressed gratitude for the apparitions article in the previous issue. We also featured a few miraculous photos that were sent in—photos that other readers had taken while at Maranatha Spring.

I then personally addressed the issue, "I highly encourage readers to consider a pilgrimage to Maranatha..." I wrote.

Father David called me immediately to discuss that particular statement.

"I wanted to call you, before the Bishop called me," he said. "I know the magazine is ecumenical, but everyone knows you're Catholic, and the Catholic Church hasn't approved these apparitions."

"I know, Father." I said.

There was a long pause. He was slow and kind with his choice of words. "There are a few red flags associated with this particular Shrine that are cause for concern for the Church."

He began to list them: "First and foremost they are unwilling to let the Diocese come in and do an investigation. And in all other legitimate apparitions, Jesus and Mary encourage seers to be obedient to the hierarchy of the Church. Holy Love Ministries, however, claims to be ecumenical and under no authority. But clearly, given their rosary services and things of that nature, they are Catholic. Also, they are promoting a special rosary, and you have to be careful with that. What makes one rosary better than another?"

I listened quietly and felt such sadness well up in me. I did not want to be having this conversation with my Pastor. I did not want him to think that I was using my position with an ecumenical magazine as a tool to be disobedient to my Faith. I didn't want to argue with him—my superior and a man of God.

Yet, at the same time, I knew deep in my soul, beyond my vocabulary, that Maranatha Spring *was* real and that I was supposed to speak out about it. The sadness was overcoming. Father paused, waiting for my response, but I couldn't give one. I began to cry.

Completely embarrassed, I muttered, "I'm sorry, Father."

"It's quite alright." He said softly and patiently.

"I know exactly what you are saying." I continued.
"In my mind, I know it well. But in my heart…" The tears were pouring now. Just pouring. "In my heart, I feel I'm being called in another direction." There was another pause. "I guess I'm in a bit of a pickle," I laughed, trying to lighten the conversation.

Father was very kind with his response and advised me to pray for discernment. He also offered to discuss things with me more at a later time, and I took him up on the offer. But the sadness remained. I did not want to be disobedient. I did not want people to think I was becoming a schismatic. Yet, I did not want to disappoint my Lord, if He wanted me to write this book, and I certainly did not want my Church to crumble in ignorance to what was taking place around it and within it.. if I could help bring things to light.

On Sunday my husband and I took the kids to Mass early and I did what Father advised. I prayed for discernment. I knelt down, gazing at the tabernacle, and I begged Him, "Lord, show me what you want me to know. What you want me to do? Please, help me to see which one is Your path and which one is not."

This particular Sunday was the 16th Sunday in ordinary time. The first reading was from Jeremiah, 23: 1-6. "Woe to the pastors that destroy and scatter the sheep of my pasture! You have scattered my flock, and driven them away…I will gather the remnant of my flock… and they shall be fruitful and increase…and they shall fear no more, nor be dismayed…"

Naturally, I thought of the problems in the Church, specifically those that we discussed from my last interview with Don, Maureen, and Fr. Mike. I also thought how coincidental it was that Maureen receives many messages, which are addressed to the "*remnant* faithful".

Truly Scripture was beginning to shed light on things. But, I was still fearful…mostly of what people would think of me. I'm ashamed to admit it. But I did not want my reputation to suffer as a result of writing this book.

Then we sang the responsorial psalm, "Shepherd me, oh God, beyond my wants, beyond my fears, from death into light." At that, I realized: persecution was a part of the journey; a very dark part. But the Lord would lead me through it. He would lead the whole Church through it, if we would follow Him.

The Gospel explained it further. It was from Mark, 6: 30-34. "…And Jesus, when he came out, saw many people, and was moved to compassion toward them, because they were as sheep not having a shepherd…"

I pictured the very sad face of Jesus that I captured in my digital camera that first time at Maranatha, and I understood why He sorrows for lost souls. It is His Love and compassion for them, "because they are as sheep not having a shepherd."

Father then began his homily. He talked about hearing God's voice, His call, and *discerning* what is God's voice and what is Satan's voice. I silently wondered, "Is Maranatha the call, the path You want for me? Or am I being led astray?"

Almost instantly after the homily, the organ began to play the Offertory song "Come to the Water". I smiled, thinking of Maranatha Spring. *"Thanks, Lord."* I thought. *"I get it now."*

I made the commitment to move forward with the book. But I wasn't *completely* content. During the Liturgy of the Eucharist, I got an uneasy feeling. Our parish no longer knelt before or after Holy Communion. They said we were to be in communion with each other. In the past, I did like the rest. I stood. But on this day, I wasn't sure I should. I recalled a couple of messages I recently read from Jesus and the Blessed Mother.

Jesus said, "If you are Catholic and listening to Me... Do not let others dictate to you your posture or demeanor in the precious moments after you receive Me in the Holy Eucharist. This is My special time with each soul and needs to be saturated with reciprocating love between the soul and Me... Do not fear putting into practice what I tell you today"

(November 5, 2003)

Our Lady then said, "As Mother, and Protectress of the Remnant Church, I cannot allow the true Tradition of Faith to fall prey to Satan's lies. Certain practices are being presented to you, My children, as favorable—even Vatican approved. The time after you receive the Sacred Eucharist is the special time between you and the Lord. Remember, in Holy Love we must love God above all else. This means He must be first. After My Son comes into your heart, it is a time for union with Divine Love. The Holy Father never asked you to stand and sing and be united with *each other* at this special moment of grace. These are all distractions. Do not be tricked into thinking otherwise. Do not relinquish this most cherished time with My Jesus to some avant-garde practice." (October 31, 2005)

Recalling this, I felt that I should kneel. I felt Jesus wanted me to. And so, I did. I dropped to my knees in a sea of standing people and Father raised the Sacred Host in the air. He said, "Behold! The Lamb of God!"

As I gazed up at Him, I envisioned the Holy Cross suspended in the air over the altar. I envisioned Jesus hanging on it, and in that moment, it felt right being on my knees in front of my God. In fact, I had a sense that *all* was right in that moment—that His sacrifice would again make me right with the Father, and His coming to me in such an intimate way would make the uncertainty right in my heart.

After Communion, I knelt down again, and put my face in my hands. I can't accurately describe what happened to me in that moment. There are no precise words, but such love surged throughout my being that I sobbed. I knew, like never before, that it was the Lord. Once again He confirmed the hand-written message Maureen showed me. Jesus embraced my heart in that communion and He was embracing my efforts to make Maranatha Spring known. It was confirmation—beyond all doubt.

A few days later, my mom came into town for an upcoming family reunion. She asked to keep the kids for a day, in order to have some alone time with them. I agreed and it seemed to be a perfect opportunity for me to visit Maranatha Spring. I had a lot of work to do on the book, a lot of things to think about, and my soul desperately needed some more quiet time with the Lord. This would be my first pilgrimage alone.

In the car, I listened to a song called "I Will Worship You With Tears" by Christian artist, Danny Oertli.

"I am broken.
I have nothing to give.
I fall at Your feet and
Worship You with tears."

I sang only the first line, then my own tears began to fall. I've heard the song many times before, but that day as I drove, it affected me on a whole new level—especially with everything that had been going on lately. The book, the new spiritual journey... everything was so humbling and so powerful. I knew I didn't deserve to be experiencing this kind of grace and it was overwhelming.

I repeated the song many times and then, in no time, I arrived at Maranatha Spring. I parked my car at the prayer center in order to walk the site. As soon as I got out of the car, however, it began to rain. First, a light sprinkle, then a downpour. I made my way to the back of the property, to the United Hearts Field where there stood the two statues of Jesus and Mary. While standing before the Sacred Heart of Jesus, I suddenly felt Him there with me. I wish I could describe it, but I can't. There was a strong emotion that just suddenly consumed me...an emotion of joy and love all mixed together.

I dropped to my knees at the foot of the statue. I bowed my head, closed my eyes and cried so hard my shoulders shook. All I could think was, "I am not worthy to be here, to have this responsibility, to take this journey. But I love you. I love you. And I will do whatever you ask of me."

I opened my eyes and saw that my hands were embracing the feet of the statue. Rain drops fell on them as I cried, and the words, "I'll worship you with tears" rang through my mind.

I wiped His feet, eternally grateful for the intimate moment that He gave me. I stood up, and with a newness of spirit, I reiterated my promise and commitment to Him. "Whatever you ask of me," I said. "I will do it." Looking back at the feet of the statue I noticed the rain drops covering them like tears from the song I had been singing almost the whole way to the shrine. I took a picture, and then looked at it in my digital camera. I wanted to remember that moment always.

I walked back towards my car and the rain began to let up. I didn't want to leave but I told my kids I would meet them for dinner at a local restaurant with Tim and my mom. Besides, I was coming back the next week for our interview. It would be only a few days before I returned.

The drive home was beautiful, non-eventful, and peaceful. The two and a half hours seemed more like fifteen minutes, and before I knew it, I was pulling into the restaurant. We had a nice dinner, then brought the kids home. Because it had gotten so late, we tucked them right into bed.

Immediately, I took my camera to the computer and downloaded my photos from the day, wanting just to recap before I drifted off to sleep. I clicked the thumbnail of the photo I had taken of the statue of Jesus' feet. It opened wide on my screen...and I gasped.

In my picture, the gray-colored cement base of the statue was bright red! The rain drops that fell on it were red also and they eerily resembled drops of blood at Jesus' feet. I sat back in my chair, staring at it. *"Why red?"* I thought. *"Why blood?"*

Instantly, I remembered the Virgin Mary's message to Maureen on November 12, 1997. She was talking to the visionary about different things that appear in various photos taken at the shrine. "Red is for martyrdom." She said.

I thought of the promise I made to Jesus just before I took the photo, "Whatever you ask of me, I will do it." I told Him.

Then, I thought about the week that I had, all the resistance I had come up against, and it dawned on me. Jesus was asking me to be a martyr for Holy Love Ministries. He was asking me to die to self—to put to death my worldly concerns, especially those regarding my reputation. He was asking me to accept the persecution that may come from outwardly speaking out about the United Hearts revelation and the truth found at Maranatha Spring and Shrine.

I didn't know it at the time but this picture would continue to speak to me—on many, MANY levels—in the coming years. It would continue to reveal more and more of what the Lord was asking of me. But in that initial moment, while staring at my computer monitor, I knew only that He was asking me to die to self.

I began to think of my first trip to Maranatha, and the Jamaican woman, who I had since come to know as Lorette. Once again, I heard her voice, "It will be hard, to do all that He asks, but with humility it is possible."

I then realized: humility is key to dying to self. If I was going to *truly* die to self, I needed to continually reenact that photo. I needed to humble myself at His feet every single day.

I recalled the experience I had while sitting at the Lake of Tears, looking up at the raining sky. Yes, He wishes to use me as an instrument, to fill me with His Spiritual Ink...but I needed to first empty myself of the world in order to make room in my soul for His Holy Spirit.

I needed to get rid of all that hinders me from being that willing instrument in His hand—all my pride, and that bruised ego I spent so much energy trying to protect.

Understanding this did not make it more *desirable*, however. I had no problem throwing myself at Jesus' feet for love of Him, but surrendering my reputation … well, that was a different story, giving me an altogether different kind of feeling.

"How on earth did Maureen and Don do it?" I wondered. *"How did they endure such slander and resistance, for so many years?"* I knew the answer instantly, recalling a message from Jesus.

"...Surrender your reputation. Then Satan cannot attack you through people's opinions... surrender the mission and its course, which stands protected and provided for through Divine grace... surrender your appearance. I look at your heart... surrender your health and well-being. I will give you what you need... surrender all your spiritual gifts and worldly possessions, making them mine. Now, as St. Paul says, over all these things put on love. Holy and Divine Love will fill—and fill to overflowing—anything you empty yourself of. You will not need to seek happiness anywhere in the world. You will be happy. This is how Divine Love comes into the soul and works, little heart. It takes dying to self and loving Me, as My Mother has been teaching you." (January 11, 1999)

On one hand, Maureen and Don have endured because they continually surrender everything. "We just do what we're asked," Don said. On the other hand, they have endured because they put on love. An indicator of this was a comment Maureen made in our last interview.

"We're praying for [Bishop Pilla] every day, still." They pray, with loving hearts, for the very ones who fight them and make them out to be frauds. And they do this, not for the sake of the mission, but for the sake of love.

At that I realized the depth of Jesus' request for my martyrdom. The request wasn't merely for the sake of my writing this book. It was for the sake of my journey through the Chambers of the United Hearts. There are no short cuts to salvation, no easier paths. I must walk the way—the long, self-abasing road that Jesus Himself walked... loving those who persecute you.

"Ugh." I thought. Through the grace of God, I have seen *what* the path is (Holy Love), *where* the path leads (union with God), and the way it is constructed (through six, difficult stages). Now, it seemed Jesus was showing me *how* to walk it: with humility and surrender to God's Will. I sat at my computer, lost in thought.

For some reason, I began to think about creation: how the wind blows, how it animates the trees and flowers. From the tiniest blade of grass to the mightiest oak, to the running waters and the moving clouds. All of creation feels the life of its Creator, and does not resist Him. Rather, it moves in conformity to His Will.

The great power of the Father's Divine Will is the very life force and energy of our world. Nothing takes place on earth that He does not will. Our hearts do not beat another beat unless He says so. Our lungs do not accept air unless He commands them to.

I began to think of the garden path through the United Hearts. I began to understand that His Will is the breeze that blows along the path. By surrendering to this wind, by conforming our will to His, we set out on a sure way. We enter into the very power of the universe. Instead of forcing ourselves to take steps, we are drawn and led by His strength. We are carried, if you will. We either walk *with* the wind, or walk *against* it. The more we surrender, the quicker we travel, and the more completely we are transformed.

At that, I understood that I couldn't <u>walk</u> this path. I had to <u>surrender</u> to it. This was the strategy of the journey.

I began to understand that the breeze of God's Will blows *low* along the path. If I tried to stand tall as I walked, I could miss it. Being at His feet, however, was the perfect position to be caught up in His Almighty power and swept away to the center of His Heart.

I knew the uneasiness I felt in my heart about writing this book was because of my pride. So I surrendered my reputation and I recommitted myself to telling this story, regardless of what would cost me.

I started to go over my notes from our last interview and some recent messages. I started to wonder if there was a "loving" way that I could explain the need for the

"Protectress of the Faith" title without actually disclosing the details of any Church scandal. I wondered if I could address the scattered flock without pointing fingers at the pastors.

How in the world could I sugar coat a bitter tale like this?

I recalled Don's hesitance to show me the newspaper clippings and I thought maybe he was right. Maybe it was just supposed to be about Maranatha Spring and Shrine, not the Diocese. I thought maybe telling people about all the scandals would turn them away from the book. Then, there was the question of whether or not to include my own personal experiences, or keep the story strictly investigative.

I made a few outlines and overview paragraphs... and I crinkled up each one and threw them into the garbage can.

"Okay, Lord," I said out loud. "How do you want me to tell this story?"

CHAPTER 9

"The Starting Gun"

"Today there is much confusion…Some judge in the name of discernment. Even My Mother's apparitions are rash-judged. It is not against canon law to visit these sites before they are investigated and found worthy."
~Jesus (April 14, 1999)

"The will of man must choose Holy Love. It is not open to debate and stands undaunted in the face of discernment. Holy Love cannot be judged, for it is the judge."
~Jesus (June 28, 1999)

"The way is strewn with obstacles, therefore you must be careful. You must be cautious, for the adversary wants to trip you up and take you off the path that I call you upon. The way you must come is Holy Love, Holy Love, Holy Love."
~Jesus (September 27, 1999)

In no time at all I was back at the Shrine for our second interview. Don, Fr. Mike and I sat down at the kitchen table. Maureen brought over a cheese tray and sat down with us.

"By the way," she said to me. "Jesus said this is to be a tell-all book."

I smiled and nodded, remembering that I had just asked the Lord how I should tell this story.

This time around, I prepared very specific questions for our interview, because I wanted to address each of the red flags that Fr. David and the others had given me. It seemed these red flags were prohibiting a multitude of souls. Many would not even consider a journey through the Chambers because of the negative "press" Don and Maureen have unjustly received.

My goal now—as a participant in the walk and a journalist covering it—was to get both sides of the story and to clarify any confusion.

Therefore, this interview with Maureen, Don and Fr. Mike was only part of the investigative process. The other part was my interview with the Chancellor of the Cleveland Diocese. I spoke to him about the same red flags, not long after my interview with Don, Maureen and Fr. Mike.

RED FLAG # 1: "It's condemned."

I began the interview with the one red flag that seemed to be the most widely assumed.

"Is Holy Love Ministries, or Maranatha Spring and Shrine, *condemned* by the church?" I asked.

"The Church is always slow to approve any apparition," Don said. "[the Chancellor] even stated this in a newspaper article. Generally, they wait until the mystic is dead and then they make a formal opinion. They basically want to see what fruits have taken place."

"The diocese has never issued a formal declaration one way or the other," Maureen said.

Fr. Mike spoke up, "And you have to be careful. There is a big difference between not yet approved and disapproved— or worse, condemned." He placed a few photocopies in front of me of various texts on the subject.

One particular one jumped out at me, taken from a book written by Fr. Herbert S.M. called *Discernment of Apparitions today,* where Fr. Herbert said, "This is especially applicable when it is carelessly and irresponsibly bandied about that, 'the Church has condemned' such and such an apparition, when only a local Ordinary, with his limited, human, fallible judgment, has pronounced that he does not have enough evidence in his mind to declare a 'supernatural' intervention has occurred."[5]

He later quoted the eminent Marian scholar, Fr. Rene' Laurentin, the most important authority worldwide on both apparitions and visionaries, who said that if Lourdes had happened today, it would not have been approved.

"Why is this?" I wondered.

Perhaps an article I recently read in *Spirit Daily* said it best. "In the scientific West, a straying from Scripture and a replacement of it with philosophy, especially in seminaries, has led to a climate that is often skeptical and even hostile to such revelations." [6]

As I listened to Fr. Mike a Scripture came to mind: "Do not despise prophesying, but test everything, holding fast to what is good." (1 Thes. 5: 19-21)

"If we could just allow ourselves to see that Holy Love is good," I thought. *"If we could just see that it produces only the best of fruits."*

Archbishop Gabriel Ganaka of Jos, Nigeria stated in his Foreword to *Holy and Divine Love: The Remedy and the Triumph*, "[These Messages given to Maureen] could not have possibly been the invention of a mere mortal...[and] Satan could not possibly call ceaselessly for love of God and of

---

[5] The Discernment of Visionaries and Apparitions Today by Fr. Albert J. Herbert S.M. Paulina, LA, 1994
[6] Spiritdaily.com/ratzingerseers.htm 10/16/2005

neighbor, for prayer and sacrifice, for holiness of life, the frequent and worthy reception of the sacraments and for the use of sacramentals..."[7]

Ironically, even the Chancellor referred to this in my interview with him.

"Many have cautioned to stay away from Holy Love Ministries because it has been 'condemned by the Church'," I said. "Is this a true statement? Has it been 'condemned' or is it just not approved yet?"

The Chancellor sighed. "Well, there's never been anything about *condemnation*," he admitted. "There's a *warning,* cautioning people that we would not encourage their participation in this, but *not* condemnation. We suggest they...stay with things they are sure about—the Mass, the Sacraments, the teachings of the Church."

The Blessed Mother later gave Maureen this message, relevant to our discussion: "...The statement 'not recommended in any way' and 'to use extreme caution' is not based on truth or fact, but on Satan's lies. It is Satan who loses when My children gather to pray... Authorities certainly need to be cautious themselves in coming against good...Today, I call upon My children to have the courage of belief in these apparitions despite unwarranted opposition. Have courage to recognize that these messages and all the

---

[7] Holy and Divine Love: The Remedy and the Triumph

143

messages given here lead to salvation and holiness. Do not let your decision concerning these miracles of grace be based merely upon titles, empty cautions, and even untruths..." (August 22, 2008)

RED FLAG #2: Obedience to the Hierarchy

I then asked the Chancellor about the messages given to Maureen.

"While there's not a great deal that is directly *contrary* to the teachings of the Church," he said. "They seem to be driving a subtle wedge between the Magisterium of the Bishop and his people."

"The *messages* were driving a wedge?" I asked.

"...they made all kinds of [accusations] about corrupt Bishops," He. told me. Here he was referring to the need for the "Protectress of the Faith" title and prayer which indicated people would need protection from heresy and schism in the latter days. "You have to be careful," the Chancellor continued. "It got into something that I've never seen in any...accepted or authenticated phenomena."

He was referring to the way Holy Love Ministries responded to the Diocese. All other visionaries have followed in obedience to the hierarchy of the Church. But this time, it was different.

In the beginning, when the Diocese did not approve Maureen's prayer request (for the prayer and title "Mary Protectress of the Faith"), Holy Love Ministries went to another Bishop and got approval. That Bishop, however, withdrew his approval and later, Holy Love Ministries propagated the prayer anyway, stating the title had received an approval in another country, which was in fact true.

In 1998, Our Lady appeared to 16 year old Patricia Talbot (in Cuenca, Ecuador). Our Lady told Patricia that She was Guardian of the Faith.

The Blessed Mother told Maureen, "The faith is under attack at this time, which is why I came to you as Protectress of the Faith and why I have been proclaimed Guardian of the Faith in another area of the world." (June 2, 1998).

Even St. Thomas Aquinas spoke to Maureen about this, later, after our interview. "Child, how twisted and convoluted is some leadership who accuse these Messages as driving a subtle wedge between laity and hierarchy when Heaven speaks only truth here. Those who want only to present themselves as blameless and perfect should look with the eyes of truth into their own hearts. Then they should look at the liberal factions within the Church, which certainly oppose the true Church authority..." (February 13, 2008)

After speaking with the Chancellor, it was time to discuss the issue of obedience with Maureen, which I will be honest, I did not want to do. I already believed she was telling the truth, and I knew this was a difficult topic for her. In order to get the whole story, however, I proceeded with my interviews.

"I know we discussed this briefly last time," I said to Maureen. "And I'm sorry to have to bring it up again, but it appears to be a big issue for many—the issue of obedience. Critics say that in all other apparitions, Our Lady has encouraged the visionary to follow the orders of their superior and the hierarchy of the Church. They argue that isn't the case here. Is there anything anyone would like to say to that?"

Fr. Mike adjusted himself in his chair and sorted through some papers. "Well, here's the thing," he said. "We *are* called to be obedient here at this site. We are called to be virtuous, holy *and* obedient. But obedience should be in accordance with the truths of the Faith *as handed down through the succession of Apostles*. Not to mention: obedience by itself, without virtue or piety, isn't obedience to *God*.

"That's why it's important that people know there are two Churches today—one run by Jesus and one run by Satan. These are not ordinary times. These are the end times.

146

The Church is suffering and will continue to do so…even more immensely. My suspicion is that at some point, it will be illegal to be Catholic. We have to make a decision: remain faithful during the trials or not. Our Lady urges us to go forward with this message so that souls are well-informed when the time comes to make that decision."

He hands me a sheet of paper with a message from Our Lady, given October 17, 2002. She said, "The time approaches when you and all those in the world will be challenged as never before. It will be a time of great perplexities, such as the world has never known. Plenty will give way to want. Necessities will be redefined. Economic systems will be extorted by those seeking power. More importantly, in this darkest of hours, faith will be put to the test by My adversary who will take religion into his own hands as a means of rising to power."

Father gave me a copy of a message from October 27, 2002. Our Lady said, "Had your country abandoned itself to Me under this most powerful title [Mary, Protectress of the Faith], whole segments of her populace would have been saved and faith upheld. As it is, error has scattered the true Tradition of Faith to the four winds…

"But I have returned to you under this title of Protectress of the Faith, and I ask that you begin once again to propagate it. Essentially, it is approved by another Bishop in another country. I am inviting you not to await approvals from high places at this time. The trials are too profound and numerous against the Faith. My little ones are overwhelmed with controversy."

He handed me another sheet. On November 7, 2002 Our Lady said, "The great apostasy of faith which I revealed to the children at Fatima is within the Church today. This apostasy, you see, reached even the highest positions within the Church itself. So, My little children, understand that because this apostasy remains clothed in goodness, it is an even greater threat to the faithful."

Father then gave me one last message concerning the issue. On November 25, 2002 Our Lady said, "When you repeat 'Mary Protectress of the Faith' and 'Refuge of Holy Love', the enemy will flee. It will be your spiritual refuge in the troubles which lie ahead. Your enemy is not a certain maniacal dictator, but Satan himself who seeks to destroy this planet and all on it. Therefore you need your Heavenly Mother's protection. Do not wait for sanctions and approvals. There is not enough time. Spread this message wherever you go."

We spent some time discussing these messages, and I was beginning to see the seriousness of what was taking place in the Cleveland diocese. It was an indicator to what is taking place in the world. Also, I began to see what a fine, though very distinct, line the issue of obedience was.

The Chancellor had nothing new to add to the issue of Maureen's obedience. "One hallmark in all other apparitions," he said, "has always been obedience to the local Bishop...But, there's none of that here."

He did, however, shed some light on the issue of obedience of the laity. "We never want to discourage anyone from praying, and if somebody asks, we **don't** say that it's not safe to go there." He admitted.

"So, you *don't* tell people *not* to go there?" I asked quickly.

"Well if they ask if they *should* go there, I'll say, 'Oh don't. Go to Mass. Otherwise, you're looking for signs and wonders.' But are you *forbidden* to go there? No. It's just if you *choose* to go, be very careful."

In defense of its Mission and its messenger, Heaven once again spoke about this issue, after my interview with the Chancellor.

On June 5, 2008 Jesus said, "Once again I remind those who will listen, that to oppose this Mission of Holy Love is to oppose My Father's Eternal Divine Will...Do not confuse obedience with righteousness... In My Mercy, in My Love, I have come to correct the conscience of those who oppose Heaven's Mission here. Do not listen to those who say, 'Jesus

149

would never address hierarchy like that!' If I do not correct, who will?'...There is no disobedience here at Holy Love. The only disobedience is on the part of those who try to destroy innocent reputations, who try to discourage prayer and sacrifice...

"I point these things out to you now, for the world in general and the Church as well, have been compromised and divided... My request for you to believe in this spiritual journey is crucial to the future of the world. For this reason, I no longer speak to you in veiled terms, but openly, so that you will grasp the desperate battle between good and evil...

"Many priests, religious—even bishops, even cardinals—have compromised the Tradition of Faith... The flames of perdition lick at their feet. Satan uses obedience as his weapon on control and power too often. Thus he has gained access to the heart of My Church. These truths need to be stated so that My innocent ones are not such easy prey to evil.

"I desire that you trust priests, religious, bishops and cardinals who follow the Tradition of the Faith—those who are close to the Eucharist, the Holy Rosary and personal holiness—those who are faithful to the Holy Father. Then you will be safe...

"My brothers and sisters while some caution you about accepting the truths of My Mission here, I your Jesus, caution you about accepting innuendos just because they come from sources within the Diocese...If I had waited for approval from the Pharisees, the entire Gospel message would have been lost forever. Here, just as in My public life, I have come to proclaim the good news of living in the Will of My Father through Holy Love."

Later, Jesus again addressed this issue of obedience, saying, "Today I am addressing some of the controversy surrounding this Mission... The Diocese claims... the messenger is disobedient. In what way and under which Canon law? Is she disobedient in calling people together to pray? Is she disobedient because she does not allow you, the Diocese, to close down this Mission unlawfully? Is she disobedient because she has a voice—a timid voice—which nonetheless speaks out against evils such as FutureChurch? Or perhaps you label her disobedient because you cannot control her... For many years—even decades—I have suffered with My messenger as she was calumnized before all, only because she was obedient to Me—Truth Itself. What you do to the least of My children—that you do unto Me." (August 12, 2008)

Later that same week, Jesus allowed the late Cardinal Sin of Manila (who served as the President of the Symposium on the Alliance of the Hearts of Jesus and Mary) to appear to Maureen. He said, "Jesus has allowed me to return to you, to state more gently for public consumption, what is in my heart concerning the persecution this Mission has undergone by this Diocese. Jesus desires that I clarify and bring to light the truth concerning their lie about your 'alleged' disobedience. The favored statement the Diocese proclaims about you and the Mission here is that they told you to 'cease and desist', and that you have not done so proves you are disobedient.

"Let's examine the 'cease and desist' statement in the light of truth. First of all, they never said that orally or in writing to you. Second, the Diocese cannot lawfully tell you to do so. I refer to Canons 215 and 216. You have every right to operate openly under these two Canons." (August 17, 2008)

RED FLAG #3: They're Ecumenical

"Holy Love Ministries claims to be ecumenical," I said to Don and Maureen, "yet some argue, given your rosary services etcetera, that you're obviously Catholic."

"Well," Don began. "There's a message from St. Thomas Aquinas that says it all. Do you know which one I mean, Father Mike?"

"Yes, I've made a copy of it right here," Father said.

St. Thomas Aquinas told Maureen, "According to the Catechism of the Catholic Church, Section 821, ecumenism is described as: Prayer in common, because change of heart and holiness of life, along with public and private prayer for the unity of Christendom, should be regarded as the soul of the whole ecumenical movement.

"To exclude Catholic prayer (the rosary) or symbols from the Ministry and ecumenical shrine would be to say Catholics must not be part of the ecumenical movement. This would be contrary to the local Bishops' efforts at ecumenism and the Holy Father's ecumenical efforts as well." (September 23, 2003)

"Stace," Don said, "Our Lady says the messages are for all people, all nations. We just do what She tells us. We're ecumenical."

Maureen nodded quietly.

"That's right." Father said. "And St. Thomas Aquinas makes that point as well, that they're for *all* people." He read another message.

"I have come to help you and all people to realize why these messages on Holy and Divine Love are indeed ecumenical," St. Thomas began. "The heart of the message— love God above all else and your neighbor as yourself—strikes at the heart of sin. Every sin is a transgression against Holy Love. Sin is not peculiar to one segment of the population. Satan tempts every heart...

"At Fatima the peace of the world was entrusted to the Immaculate Heart of Mary. Please note this was not the peace of the Catholic world, but the whole world. Since the Immaculate Heart of Mary is Holy Love, understand that the peace *of the world* has been entrusted to Holy Love." (December 19, 2003)

We discussed this a little further but it was those messages from St. Thomas Aquinas, as Don mentioned, that said it best. And while it sounded simple and straightforward to *me*, the Chancellor had much that he objected to.

"Another red flag," I said to him, "is that Holy Love Ministries claims to be ecumenical. Please help me understand why this is a red flag...Doesn't the Catholic Church try to foster ecumenical efforts?"

"Well," the Chancellor started, "there's no such thing as an umbrella of ecumenism. Ecumenism is a connection between Christian Churches...There is an ecumenical ministry of the Catholic Church, of the Episcopalian church, or the Presbyterian Church. But there's just not an ecumenical reality that exists all by itself."

"So you're saying that they should be part of some larger entity?" I asked.

"Right." He agreed. "And if all of the things that they are doing are associated with the Catholic Church, then they ought to talk to the Bishop about that."

"If they were part of an ecumenical ministry of a Presbyterian Church or something," I said. "Would it be more likely, that they would be looked at, and not 'warned against', by the Catholic Church?"

"Well, that would be difficult to say because one of the differences is...the Presbyterians don't have a central teaching authority (or hierarchy) like the Catholic Church does. The local Bishop would have authority, and..." He paused. "Most other Churches aren't set up in that kind of way; they don't have an authority."

"I'm confused," I admitted. "How then is an ecumenical ministry *ever* validated by the Catholic Church or not 'warned against', if they aren't Catholic and no other Church has an authority to authenticate it?"

"They just start out from there!" He said, a little irritated with my lack of understanding. "If they have a Catholic background they're Catholic...again, ecumenism is a connection between; it's not an umbrella over. They don't have a separate existence."

I still wasn't following him. As the Editor for an ecumenical magazine—that is not a ministry of solely one Church—I didn't understand why there couldn't be organizations (not Churches) that served as a "connection between" all Churches, as he said.

But at this point our conversation was getting a little too heated for my liking, considering he was a priest and an authority in my own Church. So, I decided to keep the peace and not push the issue any further.

Luckily, however, Heaven *did* push the issue. Awhile after this interview, Jesus told Maureen, "The Diocese claims we do not have a right to call ourselves 'ecumenical' since we say Catholic prayers. The Church itself is universal, all-embracing. The Holy Father is ecumenical and encourages ecumenism. The messages are for all people and all nations. We have the freedom under the Constitution to gather and pray as we choose. We are also protected in this right under Canon Law (215 and 216). I am asking the Diocesan officials who accuse us unjustly in the matter of our ecumenical status to refrain from using their authority in the manner of a police state." (August 12, 2008)

St. Thomas Aquinas also spoke to Maureen about this. "Today I have come to help the world to see that what opposes this Ministry speaks of the times in which you live. In Jesus' day, it was the Pharisees who opposed His message of love. In these days, it is the same pharisaical spirit that opposes these Messages of Holy and Divine Love. How sad that such a treasure—such a simple solution to earth's woes—should be summarily dismissed.

"The very ones who should embrace this Mission are opposing it. Satan has inspired them to use the terms 'ecumenical' against us. Yet, the Holy Father himself is in support of ecumenism. Their real motive is to destroy, not to investigate through discernment inspired by the Holy Spirit...We must continue to be ecumenical until Jesus returns in victory." (January 28, 2008)

Certainly, when I set up this interview with the Chancellor my intention was not to make waves but rather to shed some light on a couple of confusing topics. I had no idea at the time, what a can of worms I would open. I had no idea what a battle this truly was.

My goal was simply to try and clarify what the central teaching authority of my Church was truly saying to the people, because there were many souls who had heard of Holy Love Ministries—who truly had gotten the invitation from the Blessed Virgin Mary—but weren't yet walking. They seemed to be stuck in place, waiting for the starting gun of the Diocese. They were listening for that "go-ahead" from authority...which hadn't been issued yet.

I see now that it *has* been issued—not from priests in the Church hierarchy as many expected, but from the High Priest Himself, the Lord Jesus, who in several instances sent His Holy Mother.

As She said to Maureen, "My daughter, the battle lines have been drawn here, that is to say, the battle between the Tradition of Faith and the Church liberals... What I am telling you is we must proceed in the midst of all this

157

controversy. Those who refuse to believe without approvals are like the foolish virgins who neglected to bring oil for their lamps. They have chosen darkness over light. Jesus is here now, working His miracles, enlightening the world with His truths. Do not wait for the Scribes and Pharisees to say you can believe. They believe in all that is superficial. Let us proceed in faith that only comes from God. I, your Heavenly Mother, desire your prayers and sacrifices now in these troubled times. Souls are at stake. Do not wait to make a difference." (August 8, 2008)

Friends, as you read this, I beg you: hear in these words the long-awaited starting gun for this journey. Be startled by the bluntness of Heaven's plea here, as it cuts through the air of confusion and uncertainty. Feel the vibration of the Holy Spirit coming on the lips of the Virgin Mother. And let this thundering sound jump-start your heart with an excitement for holiness and sanctity.

Lastly, begin to act at the sound of this starting gun. Do not stand idle at the starting line. Do not wait for another shot. Begin, in this present moment, to move forward into the Chambers of the United Hearts, to the center of the Kingdom of God.

CHAPTER 10

"The Hurdles"

"Those who fear the impact of these apparitions here have spread malicious lies about their authenticity—lies that cannot, and will not, be justified in righteousness. Stop and think, My little children, who would oppose messages that lead you deep into holiness, deep into the Divine Heart of My Son? Who is the enemy of love and does not want your salvation? Who inspires you to doubt the path your Mother calls you upon? If you are wise, you will see Satan's fingerprints on all these attacks, lies and innuendos."
~Blessed Mother (September 15, 2006)

"Satan will no longer contend with holiness and Christ will resume His place at the center of the universe. You do not have to understand theology to know that this is a wonderful plan and reward for all who persevere."
~Blessed Mother (August 6, 1997)

"These days, Satan attacks on every side with compromise and change, and tries to lead you away from the Holy Father, but I am calling you back to the Eternal Love..."
~Blessed Mother (October 13, 1994)

After hearing the Chancellor say that the shrine was not "condemned," I was jolted yet again, as if a real bang had just gone off in my soul. My excitement increased exponentially for the marathon that Heaven has graciously sponsored here on earth. My heart began to run, to soar forward. As the interviews continued, however, my enthusiasm slowed, with a few intimidating hurdles (also known as the remaining "red flags").

RED FLAG #4: The Rosary of the Unborn

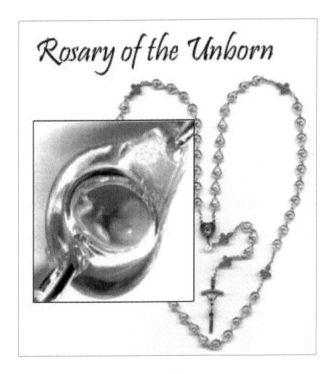

Each bead on the Rosary of the Unborn is a clear, blue teardrop. Inside the tear sits a small replica of a fetus, just as it would inside a mother's womb. And each Our Father bead resembles drops of blood, in the form of a small cross.

The design was shown to Maureen by the Blessed Mother Herself. Mary and Jesus then promised several graces available through this rosary.

Our Lady said, "I affirm to you, my daughter, that each 'Hail Mary' prayed from a loving heart will rescue one of these innocent lives from death by abortion." (July 2, 2001)

A month later Jesus came to Maureen and stated: "Every rosary prayed from the heart to its completion on these beads mitigates the punishment as yet withstanding for the sin of abortion." (August 3, 2001)

Later that day, Maureen was pondering what Jesus meant by 'punishment'. He came to her, smiled and said, "I am your Jesus, born incarnate. I know your question. Do not bother to speak it. When I say 'punishment as yet withstanding'...I mean the punishment each soul deserves for taking part in this sin. Then too, I also refer to the greater punishment that awaits the world for embracing this sin."

For some reason this rosary was a major red flag for many. So I asked the question to Don, Maureen and Father Mike. "You're promoting the new rosary of the unborn here," I said, "and with it, special promises relevant only to this

161

rosary. But critics argue 'what makes one rosary better than any other?'"

"First," Don said, "the design for this rosary was shown to Maureen on the Feast of the Most Holy Rosary. She told us to get working on them, but it was hard. Very few people wanted to even try because they were so detailed, with the fetuses and all. Then we had someone who tried to steal the design...it was one thing after another. But five years later, the rosaries were finally completed. And it was at that time—after they were done—that Our Lady gave Maureen the promises attached to them."

"This is a very serious sin," Father noted. "People don't realize this." He searches through his stack of papers. "Let me read you a message from Jesus from just the other day. He says, 'I am your Jesus, born Incarnate. Today, I have come to help each one realize the profound influence that every abortion has upon the world. When the gift of life is violated in the womb, the world moves closer to the edge of the abyss, and the abyss itself between Heaven and earth widens.

"All of the gifts—spiritual, mental and physical that were bestowed on that innocent life at conception—are killed when the life is taken. All the positive effects that the new life would have had in the world are taken away with the life itself. In their place evil is made more powerful."

Father continued reading the message: "Do not wonder then, at the intensity of wars, famine and disease in the world today. Perverse and convoluted hearts have been allowed to come to power because of abortion. You have been given the weapon to oppose this terrible sin, which is a blight upon the heart of humanity, in the Rosary of the Unborn. Do not put it down." (August 13, 2006)

Father Mike picks up another paper. "Then later that same day, at the rosary service, Jesus said, 'Today, my brothers and sisters, you fear—and with good cause—the event of a nuclear war...because of nuclear fallout...and yet I tell you, that the fallout from praying the Rosary of the Unborn is much more powerful than any nuclear bomb. You will not have an end to these threats against world peace until abortion is eliminated."

"And here's one from May 11, 2002," Father said, "the eve of Mother's Day. Blessed Mother came as Our Lady of Fatima and said, 'For I tell you, a great threat awaits the world—a chastisement greater than you suffered in this country in September. It is coming, My children, unless the Heart of My Beloved Son can be appeased, for the great sin of abortion.'"

We all sat there in silence for a moment. It was a very sobering message indeed, shedding light on not only the power of prayer, but also the gravity of the consequences of abortion—not only for the innocent child's mother and father, but also mankind as a whole.

"I've said it before, and I'll say it again," Don noted. "We just do what we're told."

This didn't sit well with the Chancellor, though.

"How does the Rosary of the Unborn help or hurt [Holy Love Ministry's] claim to be authentic?" I asked him.

"Well, I have a devotional here," he said, reading to me the promises attached to the rosary of the unborn. "Now, one of the difficulties is, it's *this* rosary that their talking about...the Our Father and Hail Mary, not from any rosary but from just *this* rosary... It's certainly not a spiritual factor that holds up to any testament of the Church."

His response didn't make sense to me. There were certainly other sacramentals that are associated with promises from Heaven.* Take, for example, the brown scapular. In 1251, St. Simon Stock, head of the then unpopular Order of Our Lady of Mount Carmel, spent the entire night in prayer to the Virgin Mary, seeking Her assistance for their Order. In the morning, Our Lady appeared to him along with the infant Jesus and a host of angels and handed him the scapular along with the following promise:

"My beloved son, receive this scapular for your Order. It is the special sign of a privilege which I have obtained for you and for all God's children who honor me as

Our Lady of Mount Carmel. Those who die devotedly clothed with this scapular shall be preserved from eternal fire. The brown scapular is a badge of salvation. The brown scapular is a shield in time of danger. The brown scapular is a pledge of peace and special protection, until the end of time." [8]

This was a promise made for the brown scapular—not the blue one or the green one—and it's widely recognized by the Church. So, it seemed to me that this was NOT the first time Our Lady had promised special graces for a particular sacramental. The brown scapular is sold in Christian gift stores all over the world.

Jesus then said more on the issue after our interview.

"I tell you, human respect is passing. In the end, it is Me you will answer to. Then it will be numbered—the souls you have turned away from this spiritual journey, the babies that were killed in the womb—because you discouraged the Rosary of the Unborn. How will you answer when truth is before you?

"...My brothers and sisters, often My little lambs become confused and travel on a path that does not lead to truth. This is because those in authority over them who should be shepherding them in the truth have chosen a life of

---

[8] *God Sent: A History of the Accredited Apparitions of Mary* by Roy Abraham Varghese, The Crossroad Publishing Company, New York, 2000, p. 74

lies. This is true in the issue of abortion where Catholic politicians are supporting abortion which is legalized. It is also true in the life of this Mission, which only desires to lead souls deep into Our United Hearts and to salvation. But those in authority whose positions demand esteem have chosen to lie about it. ...Today I invite you to see that in any issue there are two sides to supporting good. First you must choose to support the good; then, you must choose to oppose evil. In the fight against abortion, you can support life by propagating the Rosary of the Unborn and by praying this rosary; but you also need to oppose abortion by informing the public of its intrinsic evil."

At this point, I felt more at ease with the Rosary of the Unborn. In fact, I felt as though I cleared that first hurdle. The problem was there was one more hurdle just up ahead...

RED FLAG #5: The Messages

I adjusted myself in my seat, a bit nervously. I admit that I did not want to tackle this last red flag. I did not want to criticize the messages—the very words that had drawn me so deeply into this journey and rekindled my love for the Lord.

"There seems to also be uneasiness regarding the content of the messages," I said to Don, Maureen and Fr. Mike. "It seems people are concerned with the length of them, which doesn't seem to fit with other, shorter messages

166

given to other visionaries. There is also concern about the fact that these messages are edited after they are received. What is your response?"

"What messages?" Maureen sighed slowly. "They always criticize the messages but they can never give an example of a specific one that they disagree with."

"We've gotten this question before," Father interjected. "It all comes down to discernment, which is also another component of being obedient."

"St. Thomas Aquinas talks a lot about discernment," Don mentioned.

"Yes, that's right," Father said, digging through his stack of papers again.

Don said to me, "You're going to need a truck to take all this home with you, Stace." We laughed.

"Here it is." Father said. "St. Thomas compares discernment to wine."

"Oh that's a good one," Don said. "He says it perfectly."

Maureen nodded and smiled.

"August 3, 2005," Father began, reading the message. "True discernment is like a gourmet palate which, when introduced to a fine wine, recognizes and appreciates the depth and richness of it. The gourmet does not make a snap judgment. Rather, he savors the wine slowly, allowing it to interact with the sensitive taste buds—a gift God has given him. There is nothing superficial about the conclusion he draws concerning the wine. He does not base his conclusion on preconceived opinions, but on the experience of his own interaction with the wine.

"How true this is in regard to spiritual discernment. So often pride is the judge, and the gift of discernment is not even present. Messages from Heaven must touch the soul. They must interact with the spirit. Like fine wine, they must be savored—their essence felt before a conclusion is drawn...People's opinions are not the same as the gift of discernment, though they may be presented as such. Beware!"

Father put the page down. "The thing is: if people really want to 'discern', they need to read the messages and allow them to seep into their lives."

He flipped to another page. "As Jesus said, October 5, 2005, 'There is no sound moral argument against this Mission if you are truly a Christian or if you say you love God and neighbor. Holy Love opposes no Christian value or teaching—no moral stand or theological doctrine. Why then, does anyone oppose it, speak, or act against it? Do not stand back and wait. I, your Jesus, am calling you."

Don spoke up. "The diocese said years ago, when we first began, that they looked at the messages—but they said they felt the messages were trying to drive a wedge between the people and the Bishop…you know because of the implications that there was scandal within the Church."

"But Blessed Mother and Jesus have said over and over," Maureen began. "They're not coming to stroke egos. There is evil in the world, even behind the Roman collar sometimes."

"Yes," Fr. Mike said. "And that's just it. No one is perfect. We're all human."

"So we're praying for them," Don said.

"Yes, we're always praying for them, especially now, as all this unfolds and they have to face what they've done," Father added.

"But at the same time," Maureen said. "We have to defend the Truth, because their lies are causing souls to be lost."

"And that's the other thing," Father said. "We're taught in seminary—well, we're *supposed* to be taught in seminary—that our job is saving souls, not protecting your property or your possessions."

"Okay," I said. "So there is no real controversy with the *content* of the messages, that is, if you're discerning the fruits. But what about the length of the messages? Some say they're too long; they're not consistent with other messages given to other visionaries."

"Well, most of the long ones are given in multiple parts," Don said. "We print that at the top of each message, right by the date it was given."

"It could be the middle of the night or early in the morning," Father explained. "And Maureen will have to get up and write something down. She might have to do this three, sometimes four times a day...or several times over a couple days. But the overall message always culminates at the time of the particular service which it is intended - for example, a midnight apparition or a rosary service, etc."

"So the messages are written down?" I asked.

"95% of the messages are dictated, word for word to Maureen while she's in prayer," Don explained. "And she writes them down on index cards. For midnight apparitions though, Maureen repeats into a tape recorder what she's being told. Then the tape is transcribed and read to the people."

"I don't go into ecstasy," Maureen noted. "That's how I'm able to write them down."

"There's a prominent Marian theologian that doesn't want to believe Maureen is authentic," Don said, "because she doesn't go into ecstasy when she sees Them. That's one of his criteria for discerning a true apparition, I guess."

"I think what he questions is the term apparition," Maureen added. "But what else are you going to call it?"

170

"Right," Father said. "They're not interior locutions...that's a whole different thing altogether.

"I still think you can have apparitions but not be in ecstasy," Maureen said. "Look at the people in Knock, Ireland."

"And look at Padre Pio, when he was alive," Father mentioned.

"Oh that's right," Maureen said. "Somebody once told Padre Pio that he had the stigmata because he thought about it a lot, that it was autosuggestion or something. Well, Padre Pio replied something to the effect of, 'Okay, then. I will think about a bull with horns and we'll see what happens.'" We all laughed.

"What about editing?" I continued. "Do you edit the messages?"

"After the message is written down, it's typed out," Don said. "Then it's sent out to be discerned by a Marian priest, before it's put on the web site. The only editing that is done is to make sure the punctuation or spelling is right. I personally, still spell like a grade school kid."

To make sure I had covered everything, I asked the Chancellor if there were other messages that were suspicious, other than the ones that appeared to be driving a wedge between the Bishop and the people.

"There are probably others, but...I don't have them written down," he said. "We haven't been monitoring them very closely...But...there seems to be an inconsistency, with things that are published and all the things that are said."

"Can you give an example?" I asked.

"I can't remember exactly," he replied.

It appeared to me, that it was just as Maureen said, "...they can never give an example of a specific [message] that they disagree with."

But to be certain, I asked the Chancellor if, in the future, he would email or fax me any messages that he found to be "inconsistent". I never heard back from him, and so I followed up with him many months later. He still did not have any examples.

We did, however, discuss some of what had been recently transpiring between the diocese and Holy Love Ministries.

"There have been many inquiries about Maranatha Spring," he said. "And so the Bishop will likely have to make a formal statement regarding the ministry sometime in the near future."

Ironically, Jesus gave a statement to Maureen also. "I have one more Diocesan allegation that I have saved until now to refute; that is, because it is so imaginative and so far-fetched. I had to help My brothers and sisters to see first the hearts of those who are placing themselves in judgment over My work here. If I was not their Savior, I would not care about their souls. As it is, I must correct them. I am their Savior. Further, all of these latest messages are given to prevent souls from being misled by authority—those I have trusted with authority.

"The Diocese claims falsely that we are 'self-authenticating'. To be true, this would mean that none of the messages were discerned by a spiritual director or advisor. *This is false.* How can anyone *presume* such a thing unless they themselves are present when each message is given? Of course they are not! My messenger has many spiritual advisors and a competent spiritual director who reads all the messages. Can the Diocese claim as much? Since her last known spiritual director, Fr. Frank Kenney, was told by the bishop (unlawfully) that he could NOT return to Holy Love Ministries, and that if he heard of him being associated with the Ministry, he would report him to the National Conference of Catholic Bishops, all of My messenger's advisors are anonymous. Wisdom dictates so.

"I believe today's messages should put to rest all of the false accusations levied against My work here. Stand with the truth." (August 12, 2008)

At the end of my interview with the Chancellor he informed me, "I don't know if you have heard, but I will be leaving this office."

"You are?" I asked.

"Yes, I will be moving to a parish."

As it turned out, the Chancellor was to leave his position the same week that the diocese would begin their federal trial, which ironically, was scheduled for the feast of the Assumption of Our Lady.

This no doubt was best for the ministry, as the Chancellor had become a big opponent. But sadly, it didn't have to be this way. There didn't have to be so much division between the ministry and his office. There didn't have to be so many obstacles along this path. If only he would have opened his heart to the messages.

The Chancellor and I finished chatting on a pleasant note and said our goodbyes. When Don, Maureen, Fr. Mike and I finished our interview, we also continued to chat pleasantly for a time. They asked me about my husband and my kids.

"Keep the video camera running," Don told me. "They grow up too fast." For a few minutes we got to know each other a little better; then Father finished with a prayer and I was on my way.

Before leaving the shrine, however, I stopped by the prayer center, still thinking about all the red flags...

I realized then, that the controversies surrounding this mission must be difficult for priests and Bishops. So, while in the prayer center, I began praying near the statue of St. John Vianney, the patron Saint of parish priests.

I prayed silently. "Please take my prayers to Heaven with you today."

I stayed there a few minutes. Then, before I left the prayer center, I snapped a photo. I looked in my digital camera and saw that the statue of St. John had its head tilted backwards, as if it was looking up towards Heaven. This was not how the statue normally looks and I knew instantly that St. John had heard my prayer... that he took it to Heaven and that Heaven was indeed looking down on *all* the Lord's priests on earth, even those who are setting up hurdles along Heaven's path.

A message from Jesus came to mind. "These last days before My triumphant return see Satan attacking all vocations—but in particular the priesthood and marriages." (November 2, 1996)

I had already given this message a great deal of thought—from the standpoint of a married woman, but what about from the standpoint of a *Catholic* woman? I began to wonder, "What is it that makes the priesthood and marriages so similar, and at the same time, so threatening for Satan?"

Instantly I knew. Satan desires the death of our planet and everything on it, and both the priesthood and marriages are life-giving vocations. A married man and woman procreate. Therefore they bring physical life to the earth. Some of Satan's fiercest attacks against this particular vocation therefore are abortion, divorce and same sex marriages—none of which produce any *physical* life.

Similarly, priests administer the Sacraments which give sanctifying grace, as well as absolution of sin, and therefore bring *spiritual* life to the earth. Therefore, one of Satan's fiercest attacks against the priesthood is to tempt a man sworn to chastity with sex—be it pornography, pedophilia, homosexuality, even heterosexual activity. Satan knows that this behavior will cause the priest to either grow dead in sin, voluntarily leave the priesthood or be excommunicated. Then there will be one less servant administering life-giving sacraments to the flock.

This is not to mention what it does for the reputation of the Roman Collar. With so many fallen shepherds, how many sheep now run from the staff—from the sacraments and the Church itself? What conniving plans the fallen Lucifer has for the precious servants of God!

This is an important thing to understand if we are to truly see the hurdles on our path. Think for one moment, about two of the hurdles facing Holy Love Ministries. The Rosary of the Unborn is the very weapon defending physical life. And the messages call people back to the Tradition of Faith, to the Sacraments, to spiritual life.

I have to admit that I felt very naive in this regard. This issue (that evil has penetrated the Church and that some priests have gone astray) was not an easy one for me to accept. But I see now that it is true. Satan has influenced some through liberality, some through heresy, some through sex... through a whole host of ugly ways.

But I came to see that the only remedy is to stand up for the Tradition of Faith, not abandon it like I had years ago. I needed to entrust the journey—and all shepherds of the flock—to the Immaculate Heart of Mary, the Protectress of our Faith. That is why She came to this Diocese! Because She wants to help.

If we do this, then *She* will make straight the path; *She* will devour the hurdles that stand in our way. I think She more than proved this when the diocese of Cleveland went to trial on Her feast day.

* In order to be considered a sacramental in the Catholic tradition, the article must be blessed by a Catholic priest.

177

CHAPTER 11

"The Pilgrim"

"The humble one is like a little child who takes direction easily, and entrusts all aspects of his well-being to his parents."
~Jesus (January 13, 1999)

"I am using the humble and little ones to confound the proud. The Pharisees today are the same spiritually as in My day. They are the smug and self-righteous who desire this Mission fit into their plans instead of their plans being transformed by the Mission. Remain a little child—always trusting that My Plans are greater than any human plan. Let me take your hand. Do not doubt My Love for you."
~Jesus (March 16, 2005)

"Dear children, tonight I come once again to remind you that My call to Holy love is a universal call to the heart of humanity. It is a call to take off the old and put on the new (Col: 3). Do not keep the letter of the law and neglect the heart of the law. Do not say that you keep the commandments yet hold contempt in your heart for your fellow man. Dear children, in all things be humble through Holy Love."
~Blessed Mother (February 6, 1997)

Coming home from the interview was like walking into a hornet's nest. The kids were buzzing swiftly around the house with an overly-irritated drone, as if to say, "Where the heck have you been, Mommy?"

I was expecting it, though, as I had been very busy with the magazine in recent weeks...and now here I was, coming in from yet another trip to Ohio. The little bees were starting to turn angrily on me—and rightly so, I suppose. I went above and beyond to shower them with kisses, but they wanted nothing to do with me. I felt absolutely horrible.

I sat down on the sofa and told them to come over and sit with me for just a second. The drone grew louder and more intense.

"Listen girls. I'm sorry I haven't been able to play with you as much lately. Mommy just had a lot to take care of with work." Their buzzing stopped and they looked at me sternly, as though critiquing my apology. "I don't like to be busy either, because I don't get to spend as much time with you. In fact, that's all I was thinking about the whole way home, 'I can't wait to see my girls!'" Anna wasn't sure she bought it.

"Really?" she asked. "You were thinking that?"

"Yep," I said. "I've missed you."

Ellie threw her tiny hands around my neck. "I knew you did!" she shouted.

"Well..." Anna said seriously, "we missed you too."

"So.... you know what we're going to do?" I asked. "We're going to have a girls day—just us—all day long."

"What are we going to do?" Anna asked excitedly.

"Well, I don't know." I said. "What do *you* think we should do? I want *you* to decide."

Anna thought for a moment. Ellie blurted out her answer, "We should snuggle ALL day!" she said.

"No, Ellie. That's boring." Anna informed her.

"Oh, yeah," Ellie said. "Right."

"Hmmm..." Anna thought. "I know! We can *all* go to Ohio!"

I was shocked at her response. I thought for sure she would suggest the children's museum or something. "Well, I don't know." I said.

"Please! We love Mary too!" Anna shouted.

"Yeah," Ellie agreed. "She's our *other* Mommy. You even said it." Their innocent and honest desire to visit to the Shrine was touching...especially since so many adults at the time wanted just to condemn it.

"And a child shall lead them," I thought. "Well, okay, if that's what <u>you</u> want." I said.

"Yay!" they shouted.

A couple of days later we packed the minivan—a stroller, a picnic blanket, a cooler, the camera, and many empty water jugs—and we headed for Maranatha Spring and Shrine.

It was a beautiful, warm, sunny day and the kids were in perfect spirits. When we first arrived at the Shrine, we went inside the prayer center. The girls looked around at all the statues, asking about each one. Then, they knelt down in front of the Blessed Mother without me telling them to. Ellie (who just turned 3 years old) was so small, she couldn't see over the top of the arm rest but she stayed there nonetheless. This was a miracle in itself for our little "live wire," as we called her.

We had a nice picnic in a small, shaded grove. Then after we were done eating, the girls sprinted across the field to the shrine at the Lake of Tears. Ellie stood at the base of the Sorrowful Mother statue, hugging it. Anna stood next to her. I watched them from a short distance.

"Mommy?" Ellie said.

"Yes, honey?" I answered.

"Not you." She told me. "This Mommy," she looked up to the Sorrowful Mother. "Mommy?" she continued. "Mommy?"

I stayed out of it.

"She's not answering, Ellie." Anna told her.

"Yeah, She must be on the phone," Ellie said.

I put my hand over my mouth to keep from laughing out loud. Both girls backed away from the statue and knelt down on the kneelers.

"Hail Mary full of grace…" they began in unison. I couldn't believe my eyes. I never once instructed them to do that; never once had we even been in a situation where they would have seen *me* do that. And I realized it was not a *cognitive* response. Rather, it was their unencumbered little souls that were divinely inspired to show respect to their "other Mommy".

We took our time at each shrine. We filled up our many water jugs at the Spring and the kids splish-splashed in the grace and hot summer sun. We said hello to the United Hearts and then Anna pointed to the white Cross at the back of the field.

"There!" she shouted.

"That's the Stations of the Cross, honey." I explained to her.

"I know," she said very solemnly. "Those are all the things that the mean people did to Jesus."

"Yes, that's right." I said.

She began sprinting across the field.

"Anna!" I called after her. "Wait! That's kind of far away!" She wasn't listening. She was running as fast as her legs would carry her toward the Cross. "I don't know if Ellie can make it that far!" She was further away now and so I picked up Ellie and ran after her. "Wait for us at the Cross!" I yelled.

She stopped like I told her, and stood staring intently at the Cross. Ellie and I caught up to her and we entered the path in the woods. We stopped at each station and talked about it in a way they could understand. Then we said an Our Father and Hail Mary as we walked to the next station. The kids thoroughly enjoyed it and so did I. To be honest, I didn't expect them to do so well... no fighting, no temper tantrums, just peace, the whole day.

We finished up our stations and headed back to the car. When we got home, we had just enough time to eat a quick dinner and go straight to bed. Ellie was nearly asleep the second her head hit the pillow. "Mommy..." she said sleepily. "I love Ohio."

"Oh...and I love *you*," I said. "Get some sleep sweet heart."

Anna was still awake when I went into her room. "Did you have fun today?" I asked her. She nodded, but her chin was quivering, as if she was about to cry. "What's the matter, honey?" I asked.

"Ohio is my favorite field trip." She said.

"I'm glad, but why the tears?"

"Well," she said, "you know how sometimes I color a heart for you with my crayons, and I give it to you, because I love you?"

"Yes..." I said.

She began to cry harder. "Well, I want to color one for Jesus but I don't know how to give it to Him."

I didn't know what to say and so I just hugged her tightly.

"Mommy, I love Him so much," she cried.

"I know, honey...and Jesus knows too. He hears you all the time, even when you just think things quietly in your mind."

"Mommy," she said. "I know it's late, but can I say my prayers before I go to sleep?" I kissed her. "Of course you can. Do you want me to say them with you?"

"No," she said, "just me and Jesus."

Tears ran down my cheeks and I left her to her prayers. I stood outside her bedroom door for a moment listening to her whisper to Jesus. I was in awe at how profoundly Maranatha had touched her.

It was late and I too went to bed. I took a book with me that I recently bought at the book store at the shrine. It was called *Liturgical Time Bombs*, by Michael Davies. Davies told the story of Cardinal Annibale Bugnini, the head of the Congregation for the Constitution for the Sacred Liturgy at the time of Vatican II. Apparently, Pope Paul VI later dismissed and exiled Bugnini to Iran though, convinced he was a Freemason. [9]

Unfortunately, however the damage was already done. Bugnini and his staff had revised the Constitution in such a vague manner that almost any conceivable future changes to Liturgy would not violate any written part of the new Constitution. In fact, his Council supported that rites be "revised in the light of sound tradition", even though the sound tradition of the Roman Rite was to "never undertake any drastic revisions", a tradition well over 1,000 years old. [10]

According to Bugnini however, the objective for the revision was to better focus on the *community*—the unity of believers—so as to adapt to the modern world. Jesus debunked this argument in a message He gave to Maureen on November 5, 2003.

In regard to the Eucharist, He said, "This moment in the interior forum must not be violated by community," He said. "Such a practice further reduces the importance of the sacrament of My Real Presence. When each soul is strengthened and nourished in this private moment with their Creator, the entire community will be strengthened."

---

[9] Liturgical Time Bombs in Vatican II by Michael Davies, TAN Books and Publishers, Inc., 2003, p. 17
[10] Ibid p. 20

Since I had started kneeling at the consecration during Mass, I became well aware of the "dangerous wake" that this Constitution gave way to. It is the Catholic belief that the bread and wine actually become the real Body and Blood of Jesus—the Body and Blood of GOD (John 6:22-59). And yet, so many looked at me with contempt as I knelt... as if kneeling before God was somehow wrong or out of place. It was the strangest thing that I had a difficult time wrapping my head around.

Maybe it's because so many just see the Eucharist as a symbol nowadays, instead of the Real Presence. Maybe the idea of God coming to us in a host is just too hard of a concept to grasp. But then, I wonder if the Incarnation of Jesus is too hard for some also? I mean, God is Spirit. He is not flesh. In the Incarnation, He became flesh to be near us. In the Eucharist He becomes bread to be in us. It's strange to me how one is embraced, but not the other.

It also saddened me, the way many in the Church have desensitized themselves to the awesomeness of the Eucharist. The numbers of Catholics who no longer kneel, genuflect or even bow before or after receiving Him. In fact, some receive Him while chewing gum, others while wearing sweat pants, even pajama pants. That's not to mention the number of women who receive Him showing cleavage or wearing other indecent attire.

Many times, Catholics use clear glass, and in some cases plastic cups to hold the Precious Blood. Some priests dispense of His body like a drive-thru Eucharist (as Jesus called it in a message to Maureen on March 11, 1998). They quickly drop Him into hurried hands, where many then swallow Him into unrepentant hearts, just before they speed out of the parking lot to get back to more important things.

What's worse: some don't even receive Him, they stick Him in their pockets where they take Him home for cruel sport, which later serves as entertainment on popular social media web sites like YouTube.

There was a reason we did not receive Him in our hands to begin with!

Some Churches have even gone so far as to move the tabernacle where He resides—from the center of the high altar to the side of the church—replacing it with the priest's chair. Or worse: they remove the Tabernacle from the church altogether and place it down the hall in a designated chapel. Yet, sleep-walking Catholics still walk into those churches and habitually bow and genuflect to an empty altar.

It is perfectly evident that we Catholics have, through "adaptation" as Bugnini called it, dulled our senses to what the term "Real Presence" actually means. And these *outward* actions are clear representations of how seriously we take the Lord's coming to us *inwardly* in our hearts. As

Our Lady said, "what is in hearts is then spilled into the world."

If someone very close to us were to pass away, would we ever consider placing their body in a plastic coffin or wearing pajamas to their funeral? It's not likely. Out of respect. Why then would we ever justify such practices at the Sacrifice of the Mass? Why would we ever put the Blood of our Creator in a plastic container or approach His body wearing such attire?

Some people object to this, I know—they say that what we do outwardly does not always reflect us inwardly. But I wonder...If Scripture tells us that at the very NAME of Jesus, every knee shall bend on earth, in Heaven and under the earth (Phil 2:10), what then should we Catholics do before His Real Presence? How has it become customary to *stand* before the God of the universe? Or what about Romans 14:11 which says: "As surely as I live,' says the LORD, 'every knee will bend to me, and every tongue will confess and give praise to God."

Picture it: The priest holds up Jesus before the entire congregation and declares: "Behold the Lamb of God!" The angels kneel. The saints kneel. The demons in hell (even the devil himself) all kneel... and yet, we human beings stand! We stand with arms folded, chewing gum, looking at our watches.

Someday we shall see and understand the tragedy that has taken place here, the abomination that we participated in through ignorance and lack of courage. I pray, though, that the Church realizes this here and now, while on earth, rather than at our judgment... when it will be too late to gather any riches from the treasury of the Holy Mass. I pray these words somehow sink down into your heart and bear fruit.

Over the years we have slowly, but surely, desensitized ourselves to the awesomeness of the Blessed Sacrament. I understand that the Congregation wanted to adapt to the ever-changing world, to make worship more appealing to society...but is it really "worship" to drag the Lord down to our changing culture? Or would we do better to rise above our comforts, in order to keep Him at His rightful place as center of the universe, and the center of our altars?

Even Cardinal Ratzinger, now Emeritus Pope Benedict XVI, was weary of this when in 1997 he said, "I am convinced that the crisis in the Church that we are experiencing is to a large extent due to the disintegration of the liturgy..." [11]

Pope John Paul II also stated, in his 2003 encyclical on the Eucharist, "Certainly *the liturgical reform inaugurated by the Council* has greatly contributed to a more conscious,

---

[11] Ibid p.37

active and fruitful participation in the Holy Sacrifice of the Altar on the part of the faithful...Unfortunately, alongside these lights, *there are also shadows*. At times one encounters an extremely reductive understanding of the Eucharistic mystery. Stripped of its sacrificial meaning, it is celebrated as if it were simply a fraternal banquet... How can we not express profound grief at all this? The Eucharist is too great a gift to tolerate ambiguity and depreciation..."

The then Holy Father went on to say, "...the faith of the Church in the mystery of the Eucharist has found historical expression not only in the demand for an interior disposition of devotion, but also *in outward forms* meant to evoke and emphasize the grandeur of the event being celebrated.

"The Apostle Paul had to address fiery words to the community of Corinth because of grave shortcomings in their celebration of the Eucharist resulting in divisions (*schismata*) and the emergence of factions (*haireseis*) (*1 Cor* 11:17-34). Our time, too, calls for a renewed awareness and appreciation of liturgical norms as a reflection of, and a witness to, the one universal Church made present in every celebration of the Eucharist.

"By giving the Eucharist the prominence it deserves, and by being careful not to diminish any of its dimensions or demands, we show that we are truly conscious of the greatness of this gift."[12]

I had been reading for quite some time when I noticed that my husband was trying to fall asleep. So I closed Davies' book and the messages on the Eucharist. I put away my scribbled notes and shut out the light. But my mind was still spinning. I began to think about the multitude of faithful Catholics who see nothing wrong with the changes to our liturgy, and it dawned on me: this is yet another reason why the Blessed Mother came to protect our faith.

"The trials are too profound and numerous against the Faith," She said. "My little ones are overwhelmed with controversy." Truly the controversy She spoke about goes beyond Holy Love Ministries, beyond pedophilia, even beyond FutureChurch, which is total dissonance to Rome. There is controversy right here under our noses, in the Roman Rite as well.

A couple weeks later, I was again packing the van for Maranatha Spring and Shrine. It was the eve of the Feast of the Triumph of the Cross and there was a midnight apparition in the Field of the United Hearts. A friend and I left at about 6 P.M. when my husband got home from work. In the car, she and I began to discuss some of the changes within the Church. I told her about two Churches I was recently at—one

---

[12] Ibid

where the tabernacle was way off to the side of the altar, and another one where it was *behind* the people in a back room.

She sighed a long sigh. "I just don't know," she said. "I mean, as long as the congregation can see it...right?" She was unsure as to how she felt about it all. And I didn't know how to respond. She was a good woman, a good Catholic, who loved the Lord deeply. In that moment, I was at a complete loss for words. This was strange because it was a topic that had been so strong on my heart recently. But here I was tongue-tied it seemed. The words had completely escaped me. So I remained quiet.

"Maybe she's right." I thought. *"Maybe it's really not as big of a deal as I thought...as long as everyone can see it."*

I started doubting everything I had previously thought, and I got really confused. How could I have been so passionate about the subject one minute and then so indecisive the next minute? Was this an attack from the enemy? Doubt and confusion, after all, were choice weapons of his. Silently, as we drove, I *begged* the Lord to somehow give me clarity on the issue, so that I was not led astray on this.

When we pulled into Maranatha, there were cars and tour busses everywhere! Security guards were even on site, directing traffic. We decided to go into the prayer center first, and it too, was packed. I stood inside the entrance looking around at all the people. A man stood out from the crowd. He was looking directly at me as if he knew me, and then began walking quickly through the crowd in my direction. He was clearly coming over to talk to me, but I had never seen him before in my life.

He held out his hand. "Hi my name is Frank," he said.

I shook his hand. "Hi, Frank. I'm Stacy." He asked what Church I went to.

I told him the name of my parish. "It's in Pennsylvania," I said.

He looked me directly in the eye, very serious. "Is the tabernacle still on the high altar?" He asked.

"Yes," I said, taken aback.

"Good," he smiled, with a genuine happiness. Then, his smile faded. "But they're moving them, you know? They're moving the tabernacles."

"Yes, I know," I said.

"They shouldn't move them," he said. "The tabernacle needs to stay on the high altar." He was looking at me...I mean, *really* looking at me, with a stare so deep I can't explain it in words. In that moment, I suddenly remembered that I named my angel from Maranatha, "Frank."

Frank suddenly looked away and began talking about other things—random things—and he did not make eye contact with me after that. In fact, his head tilted to the side a little and I realized that Frank was mentally challenged.

My friend made her way back over to us, and Frank wandered away. "Do you want to head out to the field?" she asked.

"Ummmm...Sure," I smiled, watching Frank bee-bop through the crowd.

"Did I just meet my guardian angel?" I wondered. *"And did he just answer my prayer for clarity?"*

We drove to the back of the property and I couldn't believe how many cars there were. We set up our lawn chairs in the field of the United Hearts. Moments later I saw Lou, a friend from our hometown. He had come with his girlfriend and they sat down behind us. I sat quietly looking at all the people.

"Stace," Lou said, tapping me on the shoulder. "Look up there. What is that?" He was pointing to the sky. I looked up at the dark, gray sky above us and noticed directly over the field, there was a large white circle hovering over the people. It looked as though someone was shining a spotlight into the sky, but there was not a beam of light coming from the crowd anywhere.

We sat gazing at the circle and the service began. A procession was led by a man in a wheelchair carrying a large banner of the United Hearts. Several others followed him with candles and other banners of Jesus and the Blessed Mother. Some Mexican women sang the Ave Maria in Spanish...and oh my goodness, they sounded like angels. I could have listened to them all night.

After the procession, Mary Ann welcomed the pilgrims to Maranatha and began to pray the Chaplet of the United Hearts, then the rosary. Her voice was clear over the speaker system, though she sat many yards away under the tent with Maureen, Don, two Bishops and many priests.

A field full of people prayed along with her. And as we began the second Sorrowful Mystery, Mary Ann asked everyone to kneel. This signified the Blessed Mother was present. Everyone got down on their knees in the wet field and the silence was deafening. People bowed their heads and I could feel the power in the air, as thousands of souls were simply there, in the moment, praying with the Mother of God.

After a few minutes, Mary Ann continued the rosary. Some people stayed on their knees until it finished. Others took their seats again. And afterwards, Mary Ann read the message that was given to Maureen (this message was given in multiple parts):

"...My children...understand that the truth is in your midst now in this Mission of Holy and Divine Love. Do not allow evil to convince you otherwise. Cling to the truth, and do not allow yourselves to be misled by darkness. You, My dear, dear children, are *children of the Light*.

"Tonight, as children of the Light, allow the Light of Holy Love to shine through you... I have received special favors from My Divine Son as He seeks to ignite all hearts with the Flame of Holy Love here tonight. In your hearts and in your lives, your Mother will place untold graces—graces you did not have before My coming to you tonight. Relationships with those around you will improve. Physical healings will abound. Stress will be relieved so that you can come closer to Jesus. Future difficulties, which have laid heavy on your hearts, will be resolved. What you doubted before, now you will believe. In all these things, remember to give thanks to Jesus, the One Who sends Me....I'm blessing you with My Blessing of Holy Love."

I smiled at Her words, "What you doubted before, now you will believe." I remembered my encounter with Frank. Then I leaned back to Lou who had been taking medication for a number of years for continued anxiety attacks.

"Did you hear that?" I asked him. "Stress and anxiety will be relieved."

He smiled and nodded. "You bet I heard it."

And he didn't forget it. I ran into Lou downtown a few days later and he was ecstatic.

"Hey Stace!" he said. "The morning after that apparition I woke up late—I was rushing around and forgot to take my pills. But I was fine all day! I didn't have one anxiety attack. And I haven't taken a pill since then! I even quit drinking coffee. I have been drinking the water from Maranatha instead."

"That's great!" I told him. "I'm so glad!"

"Hey, I was nervous about going there," he admitted. "I mean, I don't know a lot about this stuff. For instance, I don't know what the Assumption is. All I know is it's a Holy Day. But I carry this everywhere." he pulled his rosary from his pocket. "Because I know it's real."

You have to know Lou in order to appreciate the beauty of his experience. There is no masquerade or façade about him—and because of it, you can't help but to smile in his presence. So much trust, honesty, joy, and simplicity.

I listened to him tell his story, and I remembered how Maranatha had touched my daughter, Anna, also; and how a mentally challenged man named Frank spoke to me about the tabernacle. I also remembered Our Lady's message the night of the apparition: "You, My dear, dear *children*, are *children* of the Light."

I finally understood why Jesus and Mary call us to be child-like. As children of God, there is an inheritance waiting for us at the end of this path. Our job is to walk to it, yes. But we can't get there on our own—not even with a topographic map. The journey is too big and we are too small.

It's as if I were to give my three year old daughter a map and tell her "Walk to the bank and withdraw the inheritance your Father left you." Could she do it? No, certainly not. Even if she could follow the map, she would get distracted. In fact, I can't imagine her making it out of the driveway (past her bike) without throwing the map down and taking a quick spin. If by some miracle she *did* make it out of the driveway, it would take her little legs longer than one day to walk four miles to the bank. And what would she do in the darkness of the night without me? How cold, scared, and lonely she would feel.

We adults like to think we're smarter than a three year old. We like to think we know the way; that we can take care of ourselves—we even think that we can adjust things along the way to make the journey more "enjoyable"...things such as Liturgy. But compared to the all-knowing, all-powerful, Almighty God, we are small, unknowing and helpless. We need Jesus to walk with us, to lead us, and we need our Mother to comfort and protect us in the darkness.

That's why we are called to be child-like on the journey. The child-like soul is the only *successful* traveler, because he is willing to surrender and to be led. Adults don't always like surrender. For some reason it makes us feel weak. Surrender makes children feel safe though.

And remember: children think, speak and act with their hearts. There can be no fake pretenses with them. A child may cry and argue that he is not sleepy as he walks, but in the face of his parents, he cannot hide the truth. A parent sees that the child is in fact, tired.

As *children* of God, there can be no false virtues with us. We may say with our lips, "Yes, Lord, I will step where you tell me." We may say that we love, that we surrender, and that we are thus walking the way, but in the face of the God, we cannot hide the truth. God sees our hearts.

Like a parent of a sleepy child, God hears us profess to know our position before Him; and He watches us *stand* in His midst, snapping our gum and folding our arms across our chests. He hears us proclaim Him the center of our lives, then watches us move Him to the side of His altar.

What a multi-faceted call it is to be child-like—to walk the path of Holy Love with our *whole* hearts; to be humble in our assessment of ourselves, honest as to our position on the path, sincere in our attempts at the journey, and submitting to the Way.

Being child-like means giving the intellect the back seat, letting Jesus drive our imperfect, crayon-colored hearts...because when the mind is not the driving force, there is no anxiety (as Lou experienced), no hesitance to step forward. There is only love, trust, and an unencumbered willingness to drop to our knees—even if we're too small to see over the arm rest.

CHAPTER 12

"The Vehicle"

"It is a simple message given in a simple way. The Confraternity is but a vehicle for putting the road map—the blueprint—into peoples' hands, not to be swallowed up by it, but to be led by it. The Confraternity calls all people and all nations into Our United Hearts."
(September 16, 2003)

"I wish today to teach you about prayer. Prayer is a refuge or weapon and a means of unification—creature to Creator. The more the soul surrenders his own will to the Will of God, the deeper his union through prayer…Then see, it is Satan that tries to keep you from praying. It is Satan who embattles your heart and tries to keep you from surrendering your will so that you can pray. No matter your course of action in any event, everything depends on God. Trust this. The soul that trusts only in himself is lost."
~Jesus (April 24, 1999)

In no time at all, I had slipped into a spiritual slump. And I knew why. I had been trying to "go it alone", trying to surrender my will on my own, trying to love my neighbor on my own, trying to resist temptation on my own, trying to understand this story and write this book, all on my own.

Each morning I woke up reminding myself to surrender, love, and resist....but it was only to end up flat on my back come evening—my nerves aching from the weight of unexpected crosses, my heart scraped up by my neighbor's sharp words, and the book...the book was suffering a standstill from unconquerable writer's block.

The little self-reminders to love my neighbor just weren't enough. I was failing miserably...and finally, I crawled to confession. The priest sat across from me listening with his hand under his chin. And when I finished my litany of failures he asked me, quite pointedly, "How is your prayer life?"

His timing was perfect, really. My prayer life had been on the forefront of my mind in recent weeks, as I had just started reading a new book from Maranatha Spring: the handbook for the Confraternity of the United Hearts.

The Confraternity is an association of Catholics and non-Catholics who consecrate themselves, through prayer, to the United Hearts of Jesus and Mary. Through some basic guidelines, they strive to live a life of holiness, to make their way deeper into the Chambers. And they commit themselves to the evangelization of the journey.

Archbishop Gabriel Gonsum Ganaka of the Catholic Archdiocese of Jos, Nigeria drafted the first Constitution for the Confraternity of the United Hearts in the fall of 1999. At the request of the Blessed Mother, the Confraternity was then officially inaugurated in the Catholic Church on the Feast of the Annunciation (March 25, 2000) by the Apostolic Administrator of the Archbishop's diocese.

It's no coincidence that this inauguration came about on the Feast of the Annunciation—the moment that brought us the Incarnation of Our Lord within Mary. The whole goal of the Confraternity is to bring about "the mystical incarnation" of Christ within each one of us—a transforming union that unites the interior life of Jesus with the interior life of the human soul.[13]

In other words, the goal of the Confraternity is to bring us into the fourth, fifth and sixth Chambers...because it is then that the Kingdom of God is present in the human heart; and when the Kingdom of God is present in another human heart, there is one more slice of Heaven residing here on earth.

---

[13] *The Handbook for the Confraternity of the United Hearts*
Archangel Gabriel Enterprises, Inc., p. 26

All this was especially interesting to me because of my recent realization that I needed strength; I needed assistance, but I wasn't quite sure how to get it. Sure, I was reminding myself to act with love and to let Jesus lead my heart...but I still didn't feel Him driving. It was as if I let go of the reins but now *no one* was driving. I spent all day running aimlessly about the path and by the day's end, I was worn out and lost.

Perhaps it was because I *said* that I surrendered my internal compass, but I never really stopped watching it. I never actually handed the keys to Jesus. I never closed my eyes and asked Him to drive. I kept one hand on the wheel and never truly entrusted my journey to His care. And like a child in the face of her Father, I could not hide this from the Lord. He knew I still wanted control, and so He did not violate my free will. He did not impose on me His desire to lead.

The guidelines for the Confraternity seemed to offer a perfect remedy for my problem. By *daily* consecrating my soul to the United Hearts of Jesus and Mary, I would *continually* hand over the keys.

This would be very hard, though. So I figured it would be best if I first gave these keys to *Mary*. Like at the wedding at Cana, She could go to the Lord on my behalf. She could polish the keys and place them into His hands more respectfully and kindly than I ever could.

On April 4, 1995 Maureen was actually shown a vision of how the United Hearts work in this way.

"After Communion I saw myself as seven years old," she said, "standing in front of Jesus seated on a throne. Our Lady was on my right. I was asking Jesus to give people the grace they need to move their wills to donate for Our Lady's Prayer Center. Then I saw Our Lady move a little closer to Jesus.

"She said, 'My Son, We do need the authority to meet and pray on that property.'

"As She spoke, I saw a light come out of Her Heart and go to the Heart of Jesus. Then a light came out of Jesus' Heart and went into Our Lady's Heart. These lights seemed to melt together and become one. Jesus said, 'It is done.'

"I have never seen Our Lady directly ask Jesus for a petition before," Maureen said.

Through Maureen's vision I understood that it is in this way, through Mary's Heart, that I essentially give the Lord (in a most perfect way) my permission to do what He wants with me—and what He wants, is to use me to love other souls, to resist Satan, and to make known the Way. I personally cannot do these things on my own, but certainly *He* can do them *through* me through Mary.

Other members of the Confraternity essentially do the same; they hand over their keys as well, and we all gather together spiritually in this vehicle—this prayer group, this confraternity...like on a mystical tour bus, driven by Jesus en route to the Kingdom. The vehicle is fashioned with faithful members, powered by prayer, and it continuously attracts other members, as it rolls over hurdles and continues on down the path.

Yes, it's possible to arrive at the destination on foot, rather than by means of this vehicle. The Lord will accompany the walking travelers, just as He does those in the Confraternity. It's just that the Confraternity has room for a limitless number of souls—and the more praying souls there are, the more power the engine has, so to speak.

Prayer was what I had been missing. It was the reason why I was feeling so worn out and failing so miserably. But the confraternity offered help and support. Through prayer, it offered strength.

As Jesus said, "Understand My call to humanity is a pursuit of personal holiness through the Chambers of Our United Hearts. The best way to travel this path—the most complete way to pursue this spiritual journey—is through membership in the Confraternity of the United Hearts. I invite not only a few, but all to comprehend this." (February 20, 2004)

While reading the handbook, it seemed the Confraternity was the answer I was looking for. But...don't think for a second that just because I recognized this, I immediately jumped on board the Confraternity-mobile. There were some prerequisites to becoming a member that I wasn't sure I could handle, and the membership guidelines themselves required even *more* dedication and prayer.

First, candidates enroll in the Secular Order of Missionary Servants of Holy Love (MSHL). And to do this, they are to prepare for three consecutive days by performing some Corporal Work of Mercy. They also are to evangelize the Holy Love Message to at least one person, and reverently receive Jesus in the Eucharist (if Catholic) or the Divine Liturgy (if Orthodox)...or do additional prayer and scripture reading if not Catholic or Orthodox.

"These three days of light will serve as armor against the three days of darkness that are to come," Our Lady told Maureen. (April 15, 1995)

The three days of darkness is a punishment and purification sent by God that has been prophesied by many Catholic seers and mystics, like St. Padre Pio (who is one of the patron saints of Holy Love Ministries), St. Hildegard, and Blessed Anna-Maria Taigi, to name just a few. It is said that an intense darkness will cover the whole earth, lasting three days and three nights. Nothing will be seen during that time. The air will be infected with demons who will appear under all sorts of hideous forms, and laden with a plague that will claim mainly the enemies of the Church. It will be impossible to use any man-made lighting, except blessed wax candles. And anyone who, out of curiosity, opens his window to look out, or leaves his home, will perish. During these three days, people should remain in their homes, pray the Rosary and beg God for mercy.

Clearly, having armor against this was desirable. But, be honest, the prerequisites seemed daunting. How could I make it to daily Mass for three consecutive days when I have work and small kids? And the bigger issue: could I really live as a consecrated member? I would have to perform an examination of conscience (a series of questions dictated by Our Lady), renew the consecration prayer, and evangelize (or pray for the evangelization of) the Holy Love message every day. The way my days had been going, I barely had time for a bathroom break or a shower...where would I find time to add all this?

Needless to say, I decided *not* to become a member. I decided it would be an impossible and irresponsible commitment on my part. I decided I would be better off continuing my journey on foot. The "vehicle" was just too much for me at this point.

But it kept creeping back into my heart.

Sitting in the confessional, I confessed my failures and I knew in that moment I received His Mercy. I knew I was wiped clean. But Father was probing me about my prayer life. He was making the same connection I read about in the Confraternity handbook—prayer and personal holiness. To me, it was Jesus asking once again, "Are you going to do it?"

I recalled the vow I made to Him in the field of the United Hearts. "I will do whatever you ask of me," I said. Clearly, I needed to do this. I went home and looked at the calendar, marking off three days where I could attend Mass, receive the Eucharist, and begin the preparation process. I made prayer cards for those prayers that are recommended, and vowed to try and pray one rosary everyday...which had been Our Lady's request at Fatima.

"My Mother prays with you when you pray the rosary," Jesus said. "Her Heart is a channel through which your prayers ascend to Heaven and grace passes back down to you. Her Heart is a connection then to God and God's grace, just as you would connect an electric light to currents...I, Your Jesus love the prayer of the Mass the most. Then I love the Rosary." (April 24, 1999)

The first few days of this new ritual, however, were more difficult than I thought. One night I started a rosary after the kids were in bed—or so I thought they were. My youngest was yelling for a drink of water before I hit the first mystery, and my oldest "had a bad dream" before I got to the second mystery. By the time I was able to continue, I was exhausted and fell asleep a few prayers into it.

I wasn't sure what to do. Mornings didn't work. The kids were up so early, at the crack of dawn. Evenings didn't work, and during the day there was so much to do with the magazine, the house and the kids.

The next evening I decided to say the rosary *earlier*. Maybe that would help. I told my husband I was going to take a bath (surely, they won't bother me in the bathroom, right?) I took my rosary with me, and I locked the door. Three minutes later, there was a loud banging on the door.

"Mommy!" my youngest yelled. "I have to go potty!"

"Honey, you'll have to use the other bathroom," I told her.

"But Anna's in there!" she said.

(Since she was newly potty-trained, I knew I didn't have time to waste.) "Okay, just a minute," I sighed, grabbing a towel.

"Hurry! Please!" she begged.

By the time she finished going to the bathroom, and we got her pants back on and her hands washed, my warm bath had turned cold. I could have probably run another bath, but it was almost time to get their pajamas on and tucked into bed. So again, I gave up.

Day after day my attempts were similarly interrupted by daily life, and I began to grow discouraged...until one night, over the baby monitor, I heard my daughter in her bedroom. She should have been sleeping at this point, and my initial reaction was to go to her room and reprimand her. But, I stopped in my tracks... there, on the monitor, she was praying a Hail Mary.

This was another "ah-ha!" moment for me.

Here I was, trying to escape from the kids to pray, and what I should have been doing was praying *with* them. What better time for them to develop a prayer routine, than when they're young. After all, it was not just my responsibility to pray and pray for them; it was my responsibility to teach them to pray and pray *with* them. Not only would it make my life easier (maybe), it would make my family stronger. To me, it seemed to be a win-win for everyone.

My husband was not as optimistic though.

"What?" he said. "You want all of us to say an entire rosary, every single night? With a three year old? That's a little much. Don't you think?"

"Come on." I smiled. "Anna knows the Hail Mary and Our Father perfectly and Ellie is getting there. She'll catch on."

"She's three," he said. "And I was talking about me. It's a little much for *me*."

"Please," I said. "It would be good for our family."

"Says who?" he asked.

"The family that prays together stays together," I smiled again.

"I don't think so." He said. "You can do it with the girls if you want; but don't count me in."

"Then it's not exactly a *family* rosary..." I reminded him.

"Listen," he said. "I *don't* want to do it. I'm sorry. I really am, but it's just not for me."

I was completely discouraged now. I could almost hear my kids, "why do we have to pray it if Daddy doesn't?"

The sadness increased as I recalled a message Jesus gave to Maureen: "So often My invitations [to pray] go unanswered, for Satan opposes prayer more than any other good. Look at the world around you. Everywhere that prayer has been discouraged, evil has taken over. In families the adversary has been able to divide, for few families pray *together*. In schools where prayer was banned, you now have drugs and violence. In government bodies instead of prayer you have legalized abortion..." (April 27, 1998)

Recalling this, I started to cry.

"Why are you crying?" Tim asked softly, "Just because I don't want to say a rosary?"

"No." I said, "Because our family isn't going to pray together."

There was a pause. Then he said, "Alright....How about if I say it every couple of days, and you and the girls can say it every day if you want?"

At this point I would take what I could get. "Fine," I told him.

That night we told the kids and they were excited about the idea of the family rosary. We didn't start with a rosary however. Instead, we said a few prayers from a small little prayer booklet Don had given me.

The first one was the Family Consecration. "Many and particular graces will be given families who so consecrate themselves in this way..." Jesus said. "Through this consecration My grace will surround you and uphold you, both in good times and in bad..."

Next, we said the Dedication of Homes to Mary, Refuge of Holy Love. "Dedicate your homes to Me, and I will vanquish evil therein," Our Lady said. (March 17, 1998)

Finally, Tim and I said the Marriage Consecration prayer. Actually...*he* read it, and I smiled, thinking of the promise Jesus made concerning the prayer.

"I am giving you this consecration of marriages to Our United Hearts because of these times. These last days before My triumphant return see Satan attacking all vocations—but in particular the priesthood and marriages. Marriages consecrated to Our United Hearts will find the way made easier...It will strengthen the soul of marriages gone stale. It will increase fervor in hearts. It will convert the unconverted who consents to pray it." (February 2, 1996)

From that night on, things were different. Tim and I began laughing more—oh how we laughed! We also began talking more, about things other than the kids and overdue bills. It wasn't like we had a bad marriage before this. Not by a long shot. But we had a "regular" marriage—busy with work, kids' schedules and life. After this, however, joy entered in a new and transforming way.

The best part though—Tim went to work after that and found a small gift box inside his office mail slot. It was from one of his customers, a local manufacturing facility. Strangely, Tim did not know a representative from the facility, but the box was addressed to him. Even more strange: he opened the box to find a rosary inside. It had red glass beads and Pope John Paul II medallions for the Our Father beads. (I have considered him my husband's special patron from that day on.)

When he got home that night he told me the story of his new rosary. "I guess I'll be saying the family rosary with you every night," he said, now convinced that there was something powerful in this mysterious string of beads.

And as for me...I started to turn our guest bedroom into a prayer room. I hung a few pictures of Jesus and Mary, and kept all my prayer books in one central location. I began to get up earlier each day before anyone in the house was awake, and I sat in silence and prayer. I was also occasionally blessed with a few other minutes throughout the day too, where I could sneak off quickly and "plug in."

As it turned out, the Lord blessed me with time. Sometimes the kids slept later in the morning; sometimes they went to bed earlier; sometimes they both took naps at the same time, and it always seemed to occur at a time when the dishes were done and nothing was pressing at that moment. What was even more miraculous was how this time changed me.

I could actually *feel* the grace that Our Lady was passing back down to me in these moments. I began to not only *handle* my life, I began to *understand* it. I began to see that I was not held back spiritually by my vocation of "working wife and mother". I was not hindered by time-consuming service to my family. I was *blessed* by it!

I had so many opportunities to feed the hungry, clothe the naked, and comfort the afflicted. I was also tested more in areas such as patience and self-denial. I was beginning to see these instances as opportunities to be with the Lord. I no longer saw my life as frustrating, exhausting or mundane... I saw it as a journey through the chambers. Every moment became important, every moment, every word.

I was beginning to see that practicing Holy Love doesn't start in the supermarket with perfect strangers (although that is an important part also). It starts at home, with the very people God put in my life. It starts when my kids are up all night with the flu, wanting constant consolation (but all I want to do is go back to sleep). It starts when my husband comes home from a long, hard day at work, wanting to have dinner and put his feet up (but all I want to do is put my own feet up, and escape my own long, hard day).

Truly the grace from Our Lady was changing my entire life. I can't say that my daily routine was becoming less busy or that I was experiencing fewer trials. But the hectic, day-to-day moments were becoming continual prayers and offerings to God, because I began to see Him in each person and each moment in my life—my kids, my husband, co-workers and perfect strangers. I began to serve Him through them, and in no time at all, I noticed my family was happier, my home was more serene and my job was less stressful.

This grace from prayer made alive in my heart the message of Holy Love that had been, to some degree, living only in my intellect and my cognitive understanding. And amazingly, by the day's end, I was not flat on my back in despair anymore. I was not aching from the journey.

Rather I was *content*. It was as though (despite the chaos) I had spent the entire day in intimate relationship with Peace Itself. I guess you could say each day was now a smoother ride—perhaps it was because *I* wasn't driving any more. I was merely riding...in the Divinely-powered vehicle of the Confraternity of the United Hearts.

CHAPTER 13

"The Light"

"The practice of making a daily holy hour brings truth to light and scatters darkness."
~Blessed Mother (December 30, 2002)

"I invite you to fall in love with Jesus in the Eucharist. When you love someone, they are ever present in your hearts and in your thoughts. You try to please the one you love. My dear children, do not leave My Son unattended in the tabernacle. Send your angels to adore Him when you cannot go yourselves. These same angels will return to you bringing many graces."
~Blessed Mother (October 17, 1996)

"These days, in the final struggle, My adversary portrays black as white and white as black...And My Beloved Son has been de-frocked of the dignity and awe due to Him in His Real Presence on the altar."
~Blessed Mother (September 12, 1993)

"Please know and understand the great consolation Jesus feels in His Divine Heart whenever you pray before His Real Presence. As He is consoled, the stranglehold that Satan has upon the throat of the world is loosened, and souls are given knowledge as to their sinful ways."
~Blessed Mother (November 25, 2006)

Since joining the Confraternity and developing a new prayer life, my life began to change. My priorities changed, my outlook on things changed. Even our family changed, as prayer became a frontal part of our daily routine.

I found myself in an unquenchable state... the more I experienced Jesus, the more I wanted to know Him. So, I began going to Adoration of the Blessed Sacrament.

Adoration is where a priest places the Blessed Sacrament (a consecrated host) on the altar in a gold holder called a monstrance, so that people can come and sit with Jesus to pray and worship Him. Some people sit in silence, some people read, some people pray the rosary or other prayers.

Since joining the confraternity, I began making weekly trips to St. Joseph's Bread of Life Community in Erie, where they had *perpetual* Adoration—24 hours a day, seven days a week. At every moment of every day, someone was there sitting with the Lord. Every time I signed in on the time sheet outside the chapel, I looked at all the names who had been there that day. I rarely recognized the names, and I often wondered about those who came in the middle of the night. I had a hard enough time getting there during daylight hours. It was inspiring, really, their dedication and commitment.

The first time I went to Adoration, though, I was attacked with many doubts. Satan tried convince me it was a useless devotion, that I would be better off staying home with my kids and getting caught up on my work. I experienced a major battle in my mind that day as I drove to the chapel, but I persevered.

When I arrived at the chapel, I noticed a white flyer sitting on a bench marked: *Free Reading Materials: Please take one.* I don't know why, but I grabbed the flyer, put it in my purse, and went inside the chapel. I knelt down in front of Jesus and was quiet in my heart. A few minutes later I took out the flyer and leafed through it, noticing immediately, an article about Pope John Paul II making a trip to Baltimore, MD.

He was scheduled to give a talk there, but wanted to go to Adoration beforehand. There was a chapel nearby that was open to the public. So, the Pope's body guards for the Holy Father went to the chapel, and for security reasons, cleared out the building. To make sure there was not anyone left in the chapel, they took dogs in with them. These dogs were specially trained to detect human flesh, in order to find human survivors in accident situations.

When the guards opened the door to the building, the dogs immediately began barking as if they had detected a human presence. They led the security team to the Adoration chapel where the Blessed Sacrament was exposed on the altar. Upon entering the chapel, the dogs laid down, bowed their heads, and cried submissively before the Eucharist.

I looked up at the Blessed Sacrament before me, and felt terrible that my doubts nearly convinced me to not come. That day, I had two books with me: *Divine Love*, *Messages on the Eucharist*, and *Conversations with Divine Love*. They were books containing messages that Jesus had given to Maureen. While reading them in front of the Blessed Sacrament the most amazing thing happened. I began to feel as though He and I were conversing directly, right there in that chapel.

I began to hear His voice in my heart. I began to fall in love with Him, more so than I already had been, and I began to understand His desires a little more.

"Look at Me in the Blessed Sacrament," He said. "Here I offer My Presence over and over—continually. How many come? How many love and respect Me?" (October 24, 1994)

"I desire people adore My Eucharistic Heart," Jesus said. "I am Jesus, born of the flesh. As I came to earth clothed in humanity, understand I am still with you clothed in bread and wine. If people really believed in Me, this chapel would be overflowing." (July 1, 1999)

I began to see Jesus quite differently in that chapel. I began to see Him as a prisoner. His only relief was the company of those who would visit Him, the love of those who would worship Him. The Almighty deduced Himself to a form even lower than flesh, and He did it so that our flesh would not only have Him *near* us, but that we would have Him *in* us. He became a form lower than flesh, a form of food, so that we might not just touch Him, but *consume* Him. Not just kiss Him, but *absorb* Him. It was not enough for Him to live *among* us. His love needed satisfied on a deeper level. He needed to live *within* us.

Yet how risky it was, to make Himself vulnerable like this to sinners. Yes, His love could be satisfied more deeply as bread, but His Heart could also be more wounded. It is easy to relate to Jesus as a baby, and to Jesus as a Man... but as a Host? It takes great faith to care for Bread this way, something so ordinary, so commonplace. As a result, Jesus—the God of our universe—is often treated as ordinary and common, or worse, merely as a symbol.

"I breathe life into [every soul]," Jesus said in a message to Maureen, "and I sustain the life as long as the Divine Will of the Father allows. In return, I ask that the soul *love Me*. I desire to be the center of the soul's life. I wish to be honored and adored in the Blessed Sacrament. I long to be recognized in this Sacred Species by all people, all nations. I do not come under the sign of bread and wine to be ignored, doubted, and even disbelieved. I am here for every soul, in every tabernacle. I am longing to be embraced by humanity. I am longing to be recognized by all, not as a symbol, but as Your Living God." (June 14, 1999)

We consume Him in the Blessed Sacrament, yes, but often, into sinful hearts. And, friends, if each little sin hurts Him... think what it does to Him to be trapped in a heart full of so much unconfessed sin. Love is trapped in contempt. Light is trapped in darkness. Purity is trapped in filth.

For this reason, the lines to the confessional should be just as long as the lines to communion, but the majority of Catholics go only once or twice a year—if that. Think if you cleaned your house only once or twice a year. Think of the "house" your bring Jesus into when you abandon the Sacrament of Reconciliation.

I was one of these Catholics who didn't go as often as I should, just the "required"
times.   That is, until my conversion—and not my conversion to the Church. I mean my conversion to Jesus, that had been taking place through the revelation of Holy Love. I came back to the Church years ago. But I was coming back to Jesus on a whole new level since discovering Maranatha Spring and Shrine. It's a shame the Diocese of Cleveland could not see the good (and life changing) fruit being born from this mission.

A few days later, on December 8th (the Feast of the Immaculate Conception), my Mom, Candy and I went to Maranatha Spring for Our Lady's promised midnight apparition. It was snowing and bitter cold, even with all my gear: two coats, thermal boots, gloves and a scarf. In fact, the wind chill that evening was twenty degrees below zero. The wind blowing across the field was absolutely bone-chilling. It didn't stop people though. Thousands upon thousands still came to Elyria, OH to pray.

While in the prayer center, I warmed my hands and feet amidst the crowd, and I thought about my journey. I thought about all He had been revealing to me lately in Adoration regarding His Love, and I prayed to go even deeper into His Heart.

Around 11:00, we walked out to the field of the United Hearts. I stood in front of the Sacred Heart statue. I closed my eyes, placed my hand on the heart and prayed again, to go deeper. Suddenly, I felt the statue give way behind my hand. I felt the chest cave in softly, as though it were the chest of a real man. It took me by surprise! Actually, to be honest, it freaked me out a little. I pulled my hand away and backed up so that others could approach the statue.

I breathed in deeply and leaned my head up to the sky. The moon was directly in front of my gaze. It was so bright that it lit up the entire field. Then I noticed: encircling the moon was a circle of bright red and orange that resembled fire.

Shocked, I grabbed Candy. "Candy, look at that moon." I said.

She looked up. "What am I looking for?"

"Do you see the moving red ring all around it. It looks like fire."

She looked harder. "I don't see any red, Stace."

I pointed in the sky. "Right there...The clouds are passing through it."

She laid her hand on my shoulder and smiled. "It's only for you." As though to say, "You don't need to explain it any further".

At that, everyone was asked to take their seats. It was time to begin the prayer service. During the sorrowful mysteries, we were asked to kneel. The Blessed Mother appeared to Maureen in all white, and gave a somber message regarding America's recent consecration to Her Immaculate Heart.

"Dear children, I come to you as My Son allows, to commemorate the event of My Immaculate Conception. This year I invite you to see that in your country (USA), a renewed dedication of all that your nation is and will be, has taken place, as it was once again dedicated to My Immaculate Conception. As this is most pleasing to My Son and His

Mother, please understand that such a dedication carries with it a grave responsibility, as well.

"My Immaculate Conception was in preparation of My Infant Son's arrival in the world. At My Conception, I was preserved free from original sin so that My Womb would be a suitable First Tabernacle for My Divine Son. In so doing, Heaven is stating that life is present at conception. The soul is present at conception. How, then, can a nation such as the sophisticated one I now appear in, dedicate itself to the Immaculate Conception, and at the same time destroy life in the womb? How can God honor such a consecration which appears good on the outside, but is compromised to the greatest degree on the inside?

"It is for this reason My Son has allowed Me to appear here tonight. Never again will there be a midnight apparition here on this date. Your nation must come to terms with the truth if it hopes to prosper and survive." (December 8, 2006)

How sobering. Jesus would no longer permit the Mother to publicly appear to us on this date. It was just like He had revealed to me earlier—the pain caused by a heart that professes to love Him yet bears the image of His Passion. The heart of America has professed to be a Christian nation, yet has passed laws legalizing the death of innocent children. We profess to love Him and yet, we've abandoned His 5th commandment. We've heard Him say, "Whatever you do to these little ones, you do to Me." But we cruelly slaughter these little ones—more than one million of them each year, in fact.

We sat in silence for a few minutes and let the message sink in. Then, before heading back to the car, we stopped at the Spring to fill our water jugs. A man came over with an empty bottle. I told him to go ahead. He put it under the funnel, and I began to pump for him. Candy smiled at me and whispered. "You know you get graces when you pump for someone else."

As I pumped the water I watched this young man hold the bottle with such great care. He was so careful and watched it flow from the spout with such faith. In that moment I prayed silently in my heart, *"Lord, if that's true, if I get graces for this...please give them to him instead. Bless him."*

When his bottle was full, he stood up, looked me directly in the eye, and smiled. "God bless *you*," he said, with a special emphasis on the word "you". I nodded, returning the smile, and in a very surreal and unexplainable way, I felt a connection to him, as if I had known him my entire life. I felt a strange warmth in my heart amidst the frigid elements. He walked away and I watched him, praying for him, until he vanished from my sight.

We then made our way through the blizzard, back to my van. Immediately I turned the heat on high and we warmed our hands and feet. Then, I noticed a white van parked near ours. It was stuck in the snow and spinning its tires. There weren't many other cars near us at this point and so I got out to see if they needed help.

A young, black man with a strong accent said, "Oh, yes, we do need help." He and I went to the back of the van and pushed the vehicle while the driver accelerated. I buried my face in my coat sleeve, (I had already taken off my scarf and gloves).

"Please help us, Lord," I prayed. "Please."

The wind blew fiercely and the van began to rock back and forth. Within a few minutes, it was pulling away from us, unstuck. The man turned and looked at me. He put his hand on my shoulder. "Thank you and God bless you." He said. In that moment I felt something for him also. I saw the Lord in him and I nearly cried with love for this stranger who I would probably never see again in my life. What a truly beautiful moment it was!

We drove out of Maranatha, and my mom and Candy rested and slept in the car. My mind was spinning in the silence as we drove, and pieces from the evening began to come together in my understanding.

Upon first arriving at the shrine, I prayed to go deeper into the Heart of the Lord. Then, I felt His Heart give way on a statue and saw fire in the sky. But the real miracle of the evening was when I felt my own heart give way, when I felt His Fire inside me—a love I couldn't explain for two perfect strangers who I knew only to be children of God.

My mom then woke up from her sleep and the two of us began to discuss the night, specifically our time while in the prayer center. "I just can't believe how different your picture is from the actual statue of Jesus," my mom said. (She was referring to the picture I took on my first trip to the Shrine, where His face was very sad.)

"I know," I replied.

"His eyes are brown on the statue and in your picture they are blue."

I looked over at her. "No, they are blue on the statue too, Mom."

"No," she objected. "I stood there, amazed, at how very deep and very dark they were. They were like long deep portals. You could see forever in them."

I was totally confused. I was positive the Sacred Heart statue had blue eyes. "The statue on the right-hand side of the prayer center?" I asked. "The statue with the red cloak?"

"No," she said, "the statue in the center, in the alcove...the Divine Mercy statue."

"Mom, there is no Divine Mercy statue at Holy Love," I told her. "Just a painting."

"Yes, there is," she said, "in the middle of the prayer center, with a kneeler in front of it."

"The statue in the middle with the kneeler is Mary, Mom." *She* now looked confused.

"I saw Jesus," she said, very seriously. "Divine Mercy Jesus."

Apparently, my mom went to the Blessed Mother and quite *literally* found Her Son. It was just like our faith tells us, "to Jesus through Mary." But even more than that, she had been praying for the conversion of a few people very close to her, so it was especially fitting that it was the Heart of Divine Mercy that met her in her prayer that night.

The day after we returned home from Maranatha Spring, I went to adoration again. I knelt before the Blessed Sacrament and it all came together even more clearly than before. That trip was, for me, a new revelation on the Sacred Heart, that could be summarized by a message the Blessed Mother gave to Maureen.

"Today, I invite My children to realize the profound depth and perfection that comprises My Beloved Son's Heart. Allow yourselves to be drawn into this Vessel of perfect Love,

230

Mercy, and Truth. Let the Flame of His Heart consume you and bring you to the heights of union with the Holy Trinity. To Him all honor and glory!" (February 7, 1998)

Love, Mercy and Truth—the three components of His Heart. While at Maranatha Spring, I had experienced Divine Love. My mother experienced Divine Mercy. We all experienced Divine Truth when, in the message given to Maureen, it was revealed to us how displeased Jesus was with America. " Your nation must come to terms with the truth if it hopes to prosper and survive," She said.

I also began to understand how all of this related to the journey. The captivating Light on the path, the light that draws souls deeper into the garden, is the Light from the fire of the Heart of God—and nowhere is the Light more present, more powerful, than in the Holy Eucharist.

Through the Blessed Sacrament, the garden of the United Hearts is opened wide for souls. Here, we are surrounded with His Light and, if we are open, filled with it. We can't help then to love him, to love God's children in Him, to pray for them, to intercede for them and to assist them. Sometimes they are complete strangers (like I had experienced), sometimes they are ones very near and dear to us (like my mother had experienced).

When we receive Jesus, truly present in the Blessed Sacrament, we are joined to Him in a way beyond our comprehension. As St. Thomas Aquinas explains: "Through the Eucharist, the Will of God is present in the world—completely, perfectly and eternally. Then, understand that the Fifth Chamber—union with the Divine Will—is offered to each one who partakes of the Holy Eucharist." (February 8, 2003)

Jesus also explained, " Understand, child, that when you receive Me under the humble form of the Holy Eucharist that you are receiving Divine Love. All of the chambers of My Heart are open to you at that moment. Yet My Majesty remains humbly hidden, visible only to those who believe." (January 19, 2000)

It was all so clear now. The fullness of the Light that is found in the fifth chamber, the very Light that transfigured Jesus on Mt. Tabor, the glory of God the Father, is available to us in the Holy Eucharist. Through the Blessed Sacrament we come in direct contact with Divine Love, Divine Mercy, Divine Truth.

When we receive communion, or visit the Blessed Sacrament in Adoration, we are like Moses who meets the Lord face-to-face, and then descends back down the mountain—with face aglow. After we meet Jesus in the Blessed Sacrament (heart-to-heart) He deposits a bit of His glory into us and we go back to our journey, back to our community with His Light. The more we visit Him, the more Light He gives, and the deeper we go into the Chambers.

This was the answer to what I had prayed for at Holy Love: how to go deeper. The answer was the Blessed Sacrament—but not *just* the Blessed Sacrament, the sacrament of Reconciliation also.

In the confessional we "clean the house" so to speak. We become a proper dwelling where the Light is not stifled, but can take full possession of us. Like Our Lady said, " Let the Flame of His Heart consume you and bring you to the heights of union with the Holy Trinity."

Therefore, remember, next time you go to Mass, next time you receive Holy Communion or go to Adoration. Remember the Light that's available to you. Understand the depths to which you can go.

"The closest any soul can come to Me is in the reception of the Holy Eucharist," Jesus said to Maureen. "Let every Mass be an advent then, in anticipation of My coming. Your perseverance in prayer and sacrifice has the power to defeat Satan and draw the human will back into harmony with the Divine. Never before in history has Heaven needed this cooperation between human effort and Heavenly grace as it does today. It is you—My Remnant—that holds back the Arm of Justice." (December 5, 2001)

CHAPTER 14

"The Transformation"

"I come to you for I want to make the world My Own. I desire to transform every heart in and through Holy and Divine Love. Many come here to see signs and wonders, and will always do so. The only sign that is important is the transformation of each heart through love. You will return to your homes and continue to experience the graces you received here today. Do not forget the most important grace: the message. All the other signs and wonders are given to you freely only to help you understand the importance of the message of Holy and Divine Love. Do not allow other things to get in the way. Knowing this, your lives should support the message."
~Jesus (September 5, 2000)

"This Flame of Holy Love, which is the First Chamber, first sheds its light upon the areas of sin in the person's life. Gradually the soul chooses to avoid these sins and to live in Holy Love. The more he chooses Holy Love, the more his free will is melted and transformed in and through the Eternal Divine Will. This transformation continues moment by moment until the Sixth Chamber when the Divine Will lives within the heart."
~St. Thomas Acquinas (May 15, 2006)

"It is not enough to believe in the Messages here. Indeed, belief carries with it the grave responsibility of becoming the Message--of becoming Holy and Divine Love through a transformation of the heart. The Message is God's Will and His Provision which leads to salvation itself."
~Blessed Mother (December 22, 2004)

I spent several months on research and outlines before beginning the manuscript for the book. Then I spent six straight months writing...early in the morning and late into the night. Finally, I finished ten chapters and immediately mailed them to Don, Maureen and Fr. Mike. They were curious as to how things were going, as I hadn't shown them even a page of the draft yet.

A few days later Don called. There was something wrong. I could here it in his voice.

"Do you have a pen, Stace?" Quickly I searched the kitchen drawer—nothing. I grabbed one of my kids' crayons instead.

"Okay, I'm ready," I said.

He began to read a private message Our Lady gave to Maureen regarding the manuscript.

"She needs to refocus," Mary said of me. "But tell her not to be discouraged. I am helping her."

I felt a choking lump in my throat and I sat down. I couldn't believe it. "Refocus?" I thought.

"Well, I'll just pray about it I guess." I told Don.

"But don't get discouraged, kiddo." He said. "Our Lady said She's helping you."

"I know," I told him. "I'll keep you posted..." and we hung up the phone.

"Who do I think I am?" I said out loud. "Writing for the Mother of God?"

My kids looked at me strangely and then went into the other room.

"I can't do this!" I mumbled.

I started thinking of all the work I put into the manuscript, and for what? Oh, how utterly clueless I was, and how useless my previous efforts have been. I had no idea how to proceed. And so, I began to cry. I sat at the kitchen table and put my face in my hands. And I cried.

"Mary, you know how worthless I am," I prayed. "Why on earth did you ask *me* to do this?" I cried harder. "Look at me! I'm discouraged! And you told me not to be. I can't even do that right!"

I tried to pull myself out of it, but every few minutes the tears would start to come again. I couldn't get it out of my mind. Then, out of nowhere, my youngest daughter Ellie came down with the stomach flu. (And there's nothing more effective at stealing your attention than a child vomiting uncontrollably.)

That night, when I tucked her into bed, I realized: I hadn't thought much about the manuscript since she got sick. I was too busy holding back her hair and changing her clothes. I smiled and thanked Our Lady, Who was in fact helping me, even to not be discouraged. Grace comes in all kinds of forms.

Later, I snuck into the guest bedroom with my rosary. I closed the door and began to pray. I was getting distracted from the prayers, though, and so I closed my eyes in order to concentrate. Instantly I had a very vivid flashback of something that happened to me long ago—something I had not thought about in many years.

I was in college, and it was in the middle of the night. I was returning home to my off-campus apartment from a nearby party. My roommates weren't home when I arrived and I went into my bedroom.

My room was a mess, clothes scattered everywhere. I leaned down and began digging through all the pockets of all the pants lying on the floor looking for something. I stood up to look on my dresser. But I was stopped in my tracks.

I had glanced in the mirror—but the person in the mirror was not me. I did not recognize myself to such a degree that it startled me, as if I had seen a stranger in my bedroom. I took a closer look, at the face staring back at me...but it was not at all who I knew myself to be deep inside.

In the mirror my eyes were light gray—the only real color in them was red, from being so blood shot. My hair was dark, much darker than before. My skin was pale, almost pasty. And my lips barely had a different hint than my face.

I stared at myself for a long while, wondering what on earth had happened to me. How did I get to this point in my life? I was partying everyday with a heart problem. I was skipping class and could not manage to keep my grades up. I had no major determined yet. I had no clue where I was going. I was merely floating from one self-destructive night to the next.

But on that night, while staring at my unrecognizable face in the mirror, I saw things clearly—I saw that what I had become was not what I was supposed to be. And so I began a search for myself.

Because I had no clue what I wanted to do in terms of a career path, I left school. I began to keep a very private journal in an attempt to figure out who I really was and what I wanted. I titled it, "The Unveiling." I was convinced that underneath this pale-skinned, light-eyed sinner there was something more.

As I remembered that particular evening, it immediately struck me that what I attempted to do all those years ago, was just now coming to fruition. I was finally beginning to see who I was—a child of God—thanks to Our Lady's assistance.

I finished up my prayers, went into my office, and sat down at the computer. I clicked open an old picture I had taken with my digital camera the first time I went to

Maranatha Spring. It was a picture of the painting of Jesus, hanging in the apparition room—the one Maureen thinks looks most like Him. I looked intently at it, and strangely, the painting in my photo began to look like me—the color of the hair, and shape of the face.

I then opened a picture of myself saved on the computer, and put this picture next to the picture of Jesus. I stared at them both. There *were* some similarities.

I then put my picture *on top* of the picture of Jesus, with the editing software I used for the magazine.

"I must be completely insane," I whispered.

I slowly faded the picture of me so that His face could shine through—and what I discovered was completely miraculous! The shapes of our faces were in fact, the same! Our noses, our mouths, our chins—even our hair was the same and lined up perfectly. In fact, if I wouldn't have plucked my eye brows, even those would probably be identical.

I sat staring at the images thinking about my flashback from college.

"That's it!" I thought. Inside this pale-skinned sinner is the Lord.

It was amazing: these photos visibly illustrated what the Light accomplishes in souls. It was a clear image of the

transformation in Christ, an image of what I started years ago—to become more than what I currently am.

This is the journey Jesus and Mary are telling Maureen about! This is the visual representation of what can happen to a soul who journeys through the Chambers of the United Hearts.

While staring at the images of me and Jesus, I began to laugh at the thought of God dwelling in me—me—the scatter-brained, sinful college dropout, who often loses her keys, loses her temper, runs out of gas, or runs out of patience. It was ridiculous really...that God would want to come so closely to such a pitiful soul.

I then began to cry—with such profound unworthiness and gratitude and love for God's beautiful purpose. I cried, and then I laughed. Then I cried and laughed again. Truly, I was a mess staring at these two melded images.

But it was just like Scripture says. "Since you have heard all about him and have learned the truth that is in Jesus, throw off your old evil nature and your former way of life...there must be a spiritual renewal of your thoughts and attitudes. You must display a new nature because you are a new person, created in God's likeness—righteous, holy and true." (Eph. 4:21-24) This Scripture reminded me of my old nature, that person who stared back at me in the mirror of my college apartment.

Also, let me make it clear. Like Saint Paul said, "I don't mean to say that I have already received these things or that I have already reached perfection! But I keep working toward that day when I will finally be all that Christ Jesus saved me for and wants me to be. No, dear brothers and sisters, I am still not all I should be, but I am focusing all my energies on this one thing: forgetting the past and looking forward to what lies ahead. I strain to reach the end of the race and receive the prize for which God, through Christ Jesus, is calling us up to Heaven. " (Phil 3:12-14)

A few minutes later, Tim came into the office. I had been upstairs for quite a bit longer than a rosary. He saw the images on the computer screen.

"OH...MY...." He gasped. "What is that?"

"Ummmm, just some pictures..." I said coyly.

"Are you putting that in the book?" he asked.

"I don't know. Maybe."

241

"It's a little controversial, don't you think—I mean, you, merged with Jesus?" he said. "You should think about this...Wow, I'm sorry, but I can't look at it anymore." He was shaking his head. "My wife looks like Jesus...with a beard. Sorry Hon, it's freaking me out a little."

I laughed. "Okay, I'll quit for tonight," and I shut off the computer.

I didn't shut off my mind, though. I kept going over it in my head, and it became even more clear after reading a message given to Maureen.

Maureen saw a large Flame form around the tabernacle which advanced towards her. She understood that It was the Heart of God the Father. This was similar to the burning bush that Moses saw. The Heavenly Father said to Maureen, "Let us give praise now to Jesus, My Son, ever present in the tabernacles of the world...

"I tell you, while there is much talk about living in My Divine Will, most do not understand how to accomplish this goal. This is why the Revelation of the United Hearts has been given to the world. The Chambers of the United Hearts are a step-by-step journey into My Divine Will and the Flame of My Heart." (February 23, 2007)

Like the Father told Maureen, "You cannot jump from the ground to the top of the ladder without climbing the ladder. You cannot jump into My Divine Will by saying you are there without surrendering to the spiritual journey first. Today there is too much talk about the goal and not enough talk about how to attain it. The spiritual journey through the United Hearts must become familiar to all." (February 23, 2007)

I began to see that the journey through the United Hearts was a journey of total *transformation*. Actually, it reminded me of the transformation of bread into the Blessed Sacrament.

While on vacation recently, we attended a church where the Deacon gave a homily on the Eucharist. He explained the Church's teaching regarding "transubstantiation". He explained that there are two components to the Host: the accidents (which are the physical attributes, like the color, the texture, etc.) and the substance (which is the "whole," the "sum total" that these attributes make up—in this case, bread.) He said that, at the Consecration during Mass, the *substance* of bread is transformed into the *substance* of Jesus, but the accidents (the color, texture, etc) remain the same.

I thought about how the mystery of the Holy Eucharist kind of illustrates what the Lord accomplishes in souls who journey through the United Hearts. The accidents of our physical bodies remain... white skin, black skin, blue eyes, brown eyes. But our substance, our very nature, is changed and transformed, step by step, chamber by chamber.

We begin in a state less than perfect, then gradually become a substance of pure holiness. We are sanctified. We truly become new creations. We come into God like a drop of water into an ocean and then we cease to exist. The free will of a soul arriving at the 5th chamber ceases to exist, like the substance of bread. God's Will completely consumes him. The old man passes away and what remains is the very life of God within him, within the accidents of flesh. "It is no longer I who live, but Christ who lives in me." as St. Paul tell us in Galatians (2:20)

Clearly, I was nowhere near the last Chamber yet— not by a long shot. But this was a glimpse of the goal. And I now understood that the manuscript I sent Don, Maureen and Fr. Mike did not accurately reflect this.

The old manuscript was a chronicling of events, but it did not discuss anything deeper. It missed the whole point of the events, the apparitions and the messages... which was the *transformation* of souls into the image and likeness of Christ.

This transformation was the sanctification of the earth. It was the Triumph of the Immaculate Heart of Mary, when each soul proclaims, "I have been crucified with Christ;

it is no longer I that live, but Christ living in me." (Galatians 2:20)

It is then, when He is present in every soul, that He is victorious in the world. This is when He takes complete possession of the earth. Some are awaiting just for that "end-time" moment, or the rapture as my Protestant friends call it, when He returns on the clouds. But we can have that now! He is coming now, in the present moment, on the wind of the Holy Spirit to the confines of your own heart!

What's more: these pictures of Jesus and I illustrated the *process*. It illustrated that this wasn't an *instant* transformation. Rather, it happens step by step, moment by moment. It was years ago (in college) that I first began this journey, but I was just now starting to make any kind of progress. Similarly, it took me months to write that initial manuscript, which now would require so many revisions. It was just like the story of each soul... constantly learning, revising and changing, until at last, the final version is perfected.

Finally, I knew what changes I needed to make. Finally, I knew how to "refocus". The manuscript was about to get a transformation.

CHAPTER 15

"The Security System"

"I am your Jesus, born Incarnate. I invite each soul to see that their home is in Heaven; that is also where their heart should be. The soul is at peace that lives this way. It is in this attachment to eternal bliss that the soul begins his conformity, and then union with the Divine Will of God. The reason souls do not pursue such a sublime goal is spiritual blindness; that is, the soul does not see introspectively. He does not attempt to see his faults nor Satan's snares. He misses the grace of each present moment. He places himself above neighbor and ahead of God. Let My coming to you be a call to the world to analyze their own hearts by means of this message."
Jesus (November 16, 2002)

" The incredible light that you now see streaming from My Wounds will someday enlighten every heart and convict every conscience. Then hearts will hunger for holiness instead of scorning it. Spiritual appetites will crave union with the Divine Will of My Father. Values will change and this spirituality will be sought after. It is then that the end will be the beginning."
~Jesus (September 12, 2000)

"This is why so much of the revelation of Our United Hearts has to do with an illumination of conscience and perfection in love. It is a mission that teaches interior reform. All the grace is given to succeed."
~Jesus (January 19, 2001)

I began the work transforming the manuscript, and it was not easy, not easy at all. At times, I thought it would be much easier to just start over, from scratch, but there were some good things in the earlier version that I thought needed to be preserved. So, I plugged away at it, cutting things out, adding things in, revising and revising. Certainly, the book was getting a "transformation," but what was most noticeable was the transformation taking place within _me_.

One night, after the kids were in bed, my husband turned on the TV. He turned on a program we had watched a couple times before. It wasn't my first choice, but I hadn't watched TV in a long time because of my recent busyness, so I gladly sat down for a rest. It was anything other than peaceful, though.

The violence, the language, the complete and utter disrespect for human beings. I was nauseous. I seriously thought I was going to throw up. How on earth did I ever watch this show before? I couldn't take one more minute of it.

"This is horrible," I said to my husband. "I can't watch this."

"Oh, alright, sure." Tim said. He began scrolling through the channels looking for something else. It was strange. I had never felt that way before. Certainly, it had never been my favorite show, but I could tolerate it.

What is happening to me? I thought.

Violent television shows that I had previously watched, now made me nauseous at the core. Immodest outfits that I had previously worn, I could not bring myself to put on now. Certain impious events, conversations, and situations that did not bother me before, now made me very uneasy.

A couple messages from Jesus explained. " The souls that pass from Holy Love into Divine Love have been convicted in their conscience..." (January 27 2000)

"My brothers and sisters, never be satisfied with where you are on your journey through the Chambers of My Most Sacred Heart. My coming to you should bear with it a conviction of conscience. In this illumination of your own heart, you should see the areas in which you need to improve in order to go deeper into My Heart." (July 27, 2001)

This "uneasy" feeling was me coming in contact with my conscience. But how could I go on like normal? I was not enjoying my former life at all. What could I do about it? Who would even understand it? It seemed my life was being completely turned upside down. Actually, it was being turned inside out.

I was spending so much time on the interior life, that I was beginning to "live from within," so to speak. Not only did I *uncover* the garden inside, I started to *live* there. Much of my consciousness, most of my waking moments, were spent either learning about Holy Love, praying about Holy Love, or weighing my daily activities and choices against Holy Love.

And let me say: when you begin to live in the interior garden, you begin to feel the breeze of the Spirit of God, and taste the sweetness of His fruit. You feel the warmth of the Light of the Son, and begin to experience new life in your soul. Therefore, you recognize immediately when you have wandered away from it all. You notice immediately the coldness, the darkness, the lack of peace that fills the outer realm.

The strange thing is, I lived in that outer realm for a long time. I see now, though, that it was a false kingdom, where self was enthroned. Back then, every decision I made was based on how it affected me. It was not "God above all else or neighbor as self". It was me and only me.

Like the Blessed Mother told Maureen, "The conscience of the world is steeped in error and serves the god of self. But I am calling you to a deep appreciation of My grace through Holy Love." (January 9, 1997)

Back then, I *thought* I was living in light. Primarily because I had never really experienced the true Light of the Son of God, so I had nothing to compare it to. I had been traveling an altogether, different road.

"Today, sadly, your nation and most countries have chosen a course contrary to Holy Love," Our Lady said. "It is a path never before accepted with such conviction and lack of conscience. It is a path contrary to life and the laws of nature given by God. The world does not see the consequences of its choices. When I showed you all the states of your nation piled at My feet in a smoldering mass, I was revealing to you the end this nation and many others have chosen. It is a consequence that causes the angels to tremble before the throne of God seeking mitigation. I myself weep for such a loss." (October 1, 1997)

Once upon a time, I traveled this road that causes the angels to tremble... The road of self. It's a phantom road, an illusion... like a pool of water in a dry desert. It is the road that bears no fruit and cannot satisfy.

At my conversion, though, I peeked my head in at the garden. Eventually, I took a step in. For awhile, I went back and forth from darkness to Light, walking the property line precariously. Prayer one minute, violent TV programs the next. Then, over time, I began to live primarily within. I uncovered a garden paradise, my home away from home, and I put down my roots.

Now, I can't go back. Well, actually, that's not true. I *can* go back to the outer realm, and have gone back from time to time (unfortunately) out of weakness... but I know immediately when I've crossed that line. My conscience has become a sort of reverse security system, or a guard, alerting me the instant I've left the property.

Perhaps Jesus described it best. " I have come to help you understand the virtue of prudence. Prudence is the conscience of your soul. The prudent person lets Holy Love stand guard over his thoughts, words, and actions. Prudence is like a watchdog which guards his territory against marauders. Prudence stands guard over the soul, monitoring its motives and actions." (January 19, 2000)

So, if it happens, if I step across the threshold into vice and sin, my conscience makes it known to me. I seek the bridge of the confessional, and I'm teleported back into the garden.

"Holy Love is the correction of the conscience of the world," the Blessed Mother said, "and the bridge to reconciliation between God and all mankind." (February 12, 1997)

Truly, the messages from Holy Love were helping me understand what was happening to me. But, I began to understand it even *more* clearly one day while on the phone with my mom. For some reason, we were talking about the house where I grew up, which was actually the property where she grew up too.

My grandparents moved her family from West Virginia to the Erie area when she was a child. My grandfather purchased a piece of property at the end of a dead end street. It was a few acres of green grass, with wooded privacy, over-looking the blue waters of Lake Erie. There was access to a sandy beach, a small stream that flowed along the property's edge into the lake. Their house was very big, with wood floors, tall ceilings, heavy oak doors, even some stained glass charm and a front porch to watch the stunning Lake Erie sunsets.

Just off to the side of their house was a tiny one-story building, much like a cabin. My grandfather used it as a guest house for family and friends that would come to visit. He even let migrant vineyard workers stay there without cost until they could get on their feet—that is, until 1975.

That was the year my parents got married. Young, just starting out, they moved into the little cabin and began to fix it up and add on, making it our new family home.

My brothers and I played for hours a day on that property. We played kickball in the yard, made forts in the woods, built tree houses in the mighty oaks, and made sandcastles on the beach. We even planted a giant, 20-row vegetable garden. It was truly a child's paradise.

Come to find out, however, it wasn't always that way.

"I can't believe I never told you this story," my mom said.

Apparently, when my grandfather first found the property it was entirely overgrown. In fact, he bought the land without really being able to even see the house because he couldn't get to it. All he knew was that it was abandoned, needed work and, according to the papers from the realtor, was big enough for him, his wife and their eight children.

When he began clearing out the land, that's when he discovered the other, small house that my parents later lived in. No one knew it was there. After more clearing he discovered a tiny well... and although it was not quite big enough to supply water to a family of 10, the cistern he uncovered at the back of the property could. After much time and much work, the land became the paradise I remember.

I remember my grandfather enjoying it that way too. I remember him sitting on the picnic table by the lake, every night, watching the sunset. I remember seeing him smile through the window of his home office as he gazed across the grassy hill. I remember seeing his peaceful figure on the shore of the lake while he fished. My grandfather loved it there, and rarely left the property. Even after he died, I still felt his presence there so powerfully.

As my mother told me this story, I began to see that the work my grandfather put into clearing that land was just like the work we put into landscaping the interior garden. His discovery of that house was an illustration of the soul's discovery of their "home" inside the garden of the United Hearts.

And that is the whole point. It's not just our home. We don't "live within" by ourselves. It's God's home too. We didn't build it, purchase it, or merit it. It was purchased by the Blood of Jesus, given to us at the moment of our Baptism. It's our inheritance, as children of God, similar to the house my mother inherited from her father.

This is what Jesus meant when He said there are dwelling places in His Father's House. (John 14:2) This is what He meant when He said if we keep His Word, He and the Father will come to us and "make their home with us." (John 14:23)

It is as Jesus said to Maureen, "Let Holy Love stand guard over your thoughts, words and deeds. Then I will find in your heart a worthy dwelling place and make My home there. I will consume such a purified heart with the Flame of Divine Love. We will be united." (May 6, 2011)

This garden wasn't designed to be a retreat garden, a vacation spot, where we visit just from time to time. It was designed to be a permanent dwelling, a *home* for God and His children. See then how important the property lines and security system are!

After my grandfather passed away, my grandmother fell ill with cancer. Before she died, the marina next door pestered her to sell her house. So as not to leave her children with any debt, she did. She sold her property to the marina. There were issues with the property lines, though, separating what was her property and what was my parents'. Therefore, after she passed, my parents spent years in legal battles trying to determine what was the marina's and what was theirs. That changed our childhood paradise substantially.

The woods where we built our forts were torn down for a parking lot. The beach was dug up for a break wall and docks. All around our house the marina staked their claim. My little brother was even harassed by a marina employee when trying to play in what used to be our yard. Without established property lines our privacy was breached and our security threatened.

Recalling this I began to understand, to a greater degree, the importance of a well-formed conscience. If the boundaries of God's Will are not clearly defined, then the garden too is changed substantially. Our privacy is breached and our security threatened. Things from the outer realm begin to come and go, entering our spirits without alarm. Things like bad TV shows. Then, the devil stakes his claim in the garden and begins to harass little lost souls.

It was clear now. As I was reading the messages from Holy Love and beginning to pray more, I was learning how to clear out the brush from the garden. I was learning how to clean myself up, how to remove sin (through confession), and how to practice virtue. In doing so, every little transgression against God or neighbor, every little weed, became more visible at its onset through the light of the Holy Spirit (whereas previously, they were rarely noticed at all, hidden beneath the thicket).

I guess this is how it's supposed to be. Living in a fallen, sinful world, it's not a problem to feel "uneasy" from time to time. The problem would be if we _did not_ feel uneasy. We can't escape the evils of the world, so our consciences should be challenged and pricked regularly. This shows progress. I had it backwards. I thought the uneasiness meant there was something wrong with me. But, it really signified a good thing.

Not only was I uncovering the garden, trying to restore it to its original beauty, I was defining the property lines. I was forming my conscience, edging out the boundaries of my actions according to the Ten Commandments.

God gave us the Ten Commandments, not merely as "rules". He marked out boundary lines. Within these borders is where His Presence eternally resides. These are the confines of righteousness and perfect Love, and if we wish to live with Him forever, we must reside within these boundaries also. Beyond these margins there is only darkness and death. His Light, His Life, His Goodness, and His Protection are nowhere to be found there.

And yes, God is omnipresent. Yes, He is everywhere. So even though His Goodness, Life, Light and Protection are not found outside these boundaries, His Wrath and His justice still can be.

It is for this reason the Blessed Mother has come to Maureen as Protectress of the Faith. She is the Protectress of the garden. This is why She comes with the message of Holy Love, because souls are lost, wandering phantom roads as wide as plains. "Wide is the gate and broad the road that leads to destruction," Jesus says. (Mt 7:13) Therefore, She has come to reestablish the property lines of the Ten Commandments and thereby activate the security system of conscience.

As the Blessed Virgin Mary said, "Dear children, follow the path to Heaven by living these Messages of Holy Love. I long to share Heaven with each one of you. Do not waste time looking for reasons to disbelieve. That is like looking for reasons to refuse a gift. Allow your hearts to come alive here on this chosen property. Feel My presence here and rejoice. Every moment is an opportunity to become more holy." (May 12, 2014)

CHAPTER 16

"The Community"

*"I am your Jesus, born Incarnate. My brothers and sisters,
come together at once as My Flock."*
~Jesus (March 4, 2000)

*"Come together as a song of praise, all you Marian groups.
You are not different but alike in My call to you. Do not look
for differences but oneness in spirit... Evening grows nigh.
Time is short and grows shorter. Unite, My children...I desire
so much to share the victory with you."*
~Blessed Mother (February 24, 1998)

*"It is through Holy Love that I pray all people will come
together under the commandments of love."*
~Jesus (December 17, 1999)

It was another cold and gloomy morning in Pennsylvania. And for some reason I woke up singing the song *On Eagles Wings*.

It's a classic for us Catholics, played at nearly every funeral service ever held. Though strangely, I hadn't been to a funeral in years. Still, I hummed it from the shower: "You who dwell in the shelter of the Lord, who abide in His shadow for life, say to the Lord: 'My refuge, my Rock, in whom I trust...'"

Later that morning, I dropped the kids off at school and I started singing again. I even went so far as to turn the car stereo off so I could hear myself sing it more clearly. It seemed the whole world faded away and I lost myself in that song. "And He will raise you up on eagle's wings, bear you on the breath of dawn, make you to shine like the sun, and hold you in the palm of His hand."

When I arrived at St. Joseph's, a woman informed me that Adoration would be held in the main Church that day. "We have a retreat going on here today," she said.

I nodded and began walking around the block to the other building. As I approached the Church I heard organ music. Something was taking place inside...something other than Adoration.

I felt out of place. "I don't want to just barge in." I thought. "What if there is choir practice or something? ...Maybe I should just go home."

But I couldn't leave. I felt so strongly that I needed to go inside. So after a few hesitant minutes I did. As it turned out, there was a funeral taking place. It was for a man named Clyde—a retired Erie fireman who I did not know at all. Yes, I crashed a funeral.

There weren't that many people in the Church. In fact it seemed rather empty for a funeral. The service was already underway, though, and so I took a seat at the very back. Suddenly, I felt a terrible sadness come over me, and I began to sob. I cried so hard I was actually making noise.

How embarrassing I thought. *I don't even know this man.*

After communion, I knelt down and sobbed even harder. I told the Lord I loved Him. I thanked Him for leading me to that Mass at that moment. Then I prayed for Clyde.

I didn't know who he was but I prayed for Him like I had never prayed for anyone. I wiped the tears from my eyes and sat back in my seat. A woman walked to the podium. It was Clyde's daughter. "My father loved the Lord so much that he went and sat with Him in Adoration from 2AM-3AM," she cried.

How coincidental. Clyde was one of the Adorers that I had always wondered about, who sat in that chapel in the middle of the night. That still didn't explain why on earth was I there, at his funeral.

261

When the service ended, I walked to the front of the Church and took a seat. Father brought out the Blessed Sacrament and I knelt down. I thought nothing, prayed nothing, said nothing....I just cried. I tried to quiet myself so that I would not be a distraction to the others, but it was no use. I felt such terrible anguish—and I felt it so strongly there was nothing I could do to control it.

For an hour and a half I was consumed with this feeling, grieving terribly for a man I never knew. Then I remembered, very vividly, a message from Jesus given to Maureen.

"When you make a holy hour [in Adoration of the Blessed Sacrament] and then recite an Our Father, Hail Mary and All Glory Be for the intentions of the Holy Father, the punishment due your sins is remitted. Or, if you offer these same prayers, but give the graces earned to a poor soul in Purgatory, he will be released." (December 30, 2002)

Ahhh...Purgatory. That obscure place in the afterlife, where souls go to obtain final purification. It's a place where souls are perfected and cleansed in order to look, once-and-for-all, on the glorious face of the all-perfect God.

This, I know, is a controversial subject among Christians. So I should probably pause for a moment. I should probably back up a bit and explain.

Some say Purgatory is just a Catholic thing (although there are many Catholics who don't believe in it anymore either). Others say Purgatory isn't in Scripture, so it must be a fictitious place.

Granted, the word "Purgatory" isn't in the Bible. But, it *is* supported and referenced. In fact, Purgatory falls into the same category as things such as the Incarnation and the Trinity...things that aren't mentioned by their current title, as we call them now today, but are nonetheless described and explained in detail in Scripture.

First, the book of Revelations says that nothing unclean can enter Heaven, nor can anyone who "makes an abomination" (has hatred or dislike), or tells a lie. (Rev 21:27)

Also, Jesus Himself said, "Be therefore perfect as you're Heavenly Father is perfect." (Mt. 5:48)

What does He mean by "perfect"? He explained this in the Sermon on the Mount. He said to pray for those who persecute you and if someone hits you give them the other cheek. And if you look at a woman with lustful eyes you're guilty of adultery.

Even more than that, Jesus said, "Everyone who is *angry* with his brother shall be in danger of the judgment...and whosoever shall say, '[you] fool', shall be in danger of the hell of fire." (Mt 5:22)

This sounds harsh, I know, but we cannot argue it. It's Scripture. We *must* be perfect to enter Heaven—100% perfect. Therefore, there has to be a purification, or a cleansing, where the friends of God who die with small sins/flaws are purified of them. And yes, the Bible does support this. In 2 Maccabees, it is written: "Thus he made atonement for the dead that they might be freed from sin." (12:46)

This book is not found in some Protestant Bibles, but it at least should have some historical worth. Through this, we see what the pre-Christian community believed. We see evidence that the Jews offered sacrifices for those who had died. And since the Jews prayed for the dead, they must have believed in a place where these prayers could help them.

There are some New Testament Scriptures that support this also. In the Gospel of Matthew, Jesus was talking about judgment and said, "Amen, I say to you, you will not be released until you have paid the last penny." (Mt 5:26) Since in Heaven there is no "penny" that needs to be paid, and in Hell no "penny" that can be paid (there is no liberation at all), Jesus must have been referring to a third place where "pennies" do account for something—a place we call Purgatory.

Also, in Matthew, Jesus said, "Whoever speaks a word against the Son of Man will be forgiven; but whoever speaks against the Holy Spirit will not be forgiven, either in this age *or in the age to come.*" (12:32) Here, Jesus confirms that some sins can in fact be forgiven in the world to come. And since nothing imperfect can enter Heaven and nothing can save you from Hell, there must be an in-between place, a cleansing period.

Let's again consider the garden.

The journey through the garden is a journey of the soul toward unity with its Creator. At whatever point in the journey that you die, the journey still continues. If your body quits (dies) in the first chamber your soul continues on through the remaining chambers toward unity with God because that is its one and only purpose, that's what it was created for.

The "continuing on" through the garden, without your body, is what the church calls Purgatory. In Purgatory there is said to be fire, because the fires of purgatory are the fires of love.

As Jesus told Maureen, "*My Mother's Heart* is the same purifying Flame that burns away all iniquity in Purgatory." (February 18, 2002) He added, "The souls in My Kingdom of Divine Love have been purified in the Flame of Holy Love, whether on earth by choosing so, or after death in

Purgatory. So in Heaven there is only perfect love." (February 19, 2002)

If scripture says we must become perfect as our Heavenly Father is perfect... If scripture says we are conforming to the image of Christ... How can we not say there is a purgatory? Purgatory is Gods great mercy for those who die without having reached the center of the garden in this life.

Without purgatory those whose bodies quit the journey prior to reaching the 4th chamber - they would be destined for Hell! Imagine a soul just beginning to explore the great garden, falls ill and dies! Should he suffer eternal misery? No, our merciful God desires the soul finish the journey, and come to Him still. So, for this reason, there is Purgatory.

There are many who say that if a soul dies at that point, it goes straight to Heaven. But that mindset would do one of two things: it would either decrease the holiness of God, for we would reduce him to the sanctity of common man, the sanctity of the first chamber. Or, it would make Scripture a lie, because the soul was not perfect as the Father is, nor was he conformed to the image of Christ.

Moreover, what would be the point to life? If you die in any state and are admitted to Heaven, why go through the "trouble" of crucifying the flesh? Why go through the trouble of clearing the garden?

Purgatory, I know, is a touchy topic for some. For others, it is just unheard of. For Maureen, however, it is an all-too-familiar subject. On July 21, 2006, Jesus came to her with a soul who had just been released from Purgatory. "I am sending this Bishop (former Bishop of Cleveland 100 years ago—Ignatius Horstmann) back to you," Jesus told Maureen, "as you were instrumental in his release from Purgatory. He will have much to say to you about the nature of Purgatory itself."

And indeed he did.

"Jesus has allowed me to return to you to help the general public understand more about Purgatory..." the Bishop said. "The heart at the time of judgment is judged according to its resemblance to the Heart of Jesus, which is perfect Love and Mercy. Anything that is in the heart at that time which obstructs love and mercy must be purged, so that love and mercy are brought to perfection. Then the soul is worthy of sharing Heaven with his Savior. Here once again, I am speaking, not of *serious* transgressions, but more so of *attitudes*." (July 22, 2006)

The soul who dies prematurely in the journey continues it, but in a more intense manner, without the body. It is as if the little soul that was once encased in the body is stripped of its buffer. Like eyes before the sun, when sunglasses are removed. Or the hand upon a burning pan, when the glove is removed.

In purgatory, the soul now stripped of the body, experiences the fires of love in a more intense and direct manner. The garden pruning that was left undone on earth is now done for the naked soul in purgatory. The weeds left growing in the garden of the soul on earth still must be pulled and uprooted. He must be detached from the entangling vines of the world before he assumes his place in paradise.

Friends, please understand, it is far easier for us to untangle ourselves in the body with the use of our faculties and free will, than it is in Purgatory. It is easier to just simply remove ourselves from the vines, because in Purgatory they are burned away. The garden is in a sense set on fire, consumed. All that was worldly burns away, all that was good and holy remains... But not just remains, it is tested and purified and beautified from the fire. Then alas, the soul is ready.   It is like the burning bush in Genesis. (Exodus 3) The burning bush as we know was God the Father. The bush was consumed with fire but did not burn. Why? Because there is nothing in the Father that is unholy, deserving of being burned. We must become the same way, where the fire of love consumes but cannot burn...because nothing worldly and susceptible to fire remains in us. Only divine things, eternal things, things incapable of destruction.

On Memorial Day in 2007, Maureen's angel, Alanus, came to her and showed her just how constant and painful the fire of Purgatory is. "Today in your country the citizens commemorate the dead by visiting cemeteries and decorating grave sites with flags, flowers and so forth," he said. "But what I have come to show you should change the outlook of all people concerning the hereafter if they enter into this vision of Purgatory with sincere hearts."

He then led Maureen, mystically, along a path which seemed to be covered with brambles. They went up a little incline and he asked Maureen to stand beside him on the edge of a rocky cliff. He motioned with a sweep of his arm, and below was a big canyon. At one end were great flames.

"It looked like people in silhouettes bobbing up and down in these flames," Maureen said. "There were loud cries for mercy and shouts of pain, but it did not alleviate the suffering."

Alanus then said, "These are the souls in greatest need of prayer and sacrifice. This is the lowest part of Purgatory—the part closest to Hell itself. Many suffer here, for no one prays for them. They were regarded as 'good'— some even 'holy'—in their lifetime, but it was all a façade. Many priests are among these poor souls, for they were not faithful to the precepts of the Church. There are those who lied about others, and destroyed their reputations. These are them."

He showed Maureen souls who were having molten lead poured down their throats. It burned holes through their necks and did not stop.

"On a ledge around this fire were many angels—more than I could count," Maureen said.

Alanus told her, "These are the guardian angels of those poor souls being purified at this level. Through all of this suffering, the souls' greatest trial is separation from God."

"I saw souls who seemed to have their flesh melting away," Maureen said. This, too, was unending."

Alanus told her, "These are the ones who were guilty of sins of the flesh."

They moved on to view the next level. "There seemed to be something like water poured down on the fire," Maureen said, "so the flames were smaller—not as intense."

Alanus said, "Blood and water from the Side of Jesus continually flow upon the souls on this level."

"The souls were suffering," Maureen said, "but all their suffering seemed more alike, and for some reason, the souls seemed more united. They had their hands raised towards an opening. They seemed to be begging for Mercy.

Alanus told me, 'They suffer intensely for not being in God's Presence.'"

They moved on to what seemed to Maureen to be a much better area.

"These souls looked more like people," she noted, "but they were gray."

Alanus said, "These are the ones closest to Paradise. They are almost completely purified. They need maybe one Mass, or one rosary; maybe one Hail Mary to enter eternal joy. So you see: decorating graves is not what souls, long deceased, cry out for. Many spend long **centuries** in Purgatory, for their loved ones think they are in Heaven. If you pray and sacrifice for these holy souls, they will assist you now and at the hour of your death. Make it known." (May 28, 2007)

Oh, how time must drag on in the midst of this pain and separation from God. A good example is a story of a religious man who lived during the time of St. Dominic.

When he was nearing death, he sincerely begged a priest friend of his to offer Mass for the repose of his soul the instant he was dead. And so, minutes after the man died the priest went to the church and celebrated Mass for this intention.

The priest had barely taken off his vestments after Mass when the deceased man appeared to him and severely rebuked him for his hardness of heart, for leaving him in the cruel fire of Purgatory for the long space of thirty years.

"How thirty years?" asked the priest, amazed. "Why, it is not yet an hour since you departed this life, so that your corpse is, so to say, still warm."

The man replied, "Learn hence, my friend, how tormenting is the fire of Purgatory when scarcely an hour seems to be thirty years, and learn too, to have pity on us." [14]

We can only suppose that this terrible and dragging agony is why Jesus told Maureen: "How much I desire that each soul be purified on earth instead of in the next life." (February 18, 2002) It is an anguish we can't begin to fathom here in this earthly dimension.

While sitting in front of the Blessed Sacrament after Clyde's funeral, I began to understand the anguish I felt.

Poor Clyde, I thought. *Is he suffering these flames?*

After my Holy Hour in front of the Blessed Sacrament, I immediately said one Our Father, one Hail Mary and one All Glory Be for the intentions of the Holy Father, and I offered, like Jesus said, all the graces that I may have earned during that hour for Clyde.

At that moment, I knew in my heart that Clyde was the reason I woke up singing *On Eagle's Wings.* He was the

---

[14] Stories about Purgatory & What They Reveal: 30 Days for the Holy Souls TAN Books, Aug. 2005 page 18

reason I was led to that Church that day. He was the reason I felt such terrible sadness.

I finished the prayers, with the hope that Clyde would be cleansed and released. Then...it was miraculous. My sadness dissipated, and I felt peace beyond words! I knew, somehow in my heart, that Clyde was more at peace too.

I slowly got up to leave. When I opened the large wooden doors that led to the parking lot, the bright sun nearly blinded me. I lowered my head and shielded my eyes.

"Make you to shine like the sun," I hummed, "and hold you in the palm of His hand..."

At that, goose bumps ran through my body. I knew the sun that shone down on me was a small glimpse of the glory that Clyde saw. Oh, how I cherished the sun that day!

Unfortunately, however, the cold, dark skies returned the next day just as I was leaving for another visit to Holy Love. My bible study group had been planning the trip for awhile. We wanted to do our next chapter on the Virgin Mary at the Shrine. We didn't cancel because of the weather, but instead braved the elements.

We bundled up in rain gear and warm clothes and went from area to area throughout the Shrine. At the Lake of Tears we walked around, meditating on the life of the Sorrowful Mother. At the Lake of Angels we read through the testimonies and took a group picture. At the Spring we filled up our jugs and then headed across the Field of the United Hearts, toward the Stations of the Cross.

The wind blew at our faces and through our jackets—but onward Christian soldiers we went. We pulled our coats, hoods and hats tightly around us and kept walking.

Until...

"Wait a minute, guys" one of the women said, stopping dead in her tracks. "Look at the grass!" We stopped and looked around.

All around us were light green hearts on the dark green grass. It looked as though someone had used a large can of green spray paint to draw them. But it was not paint. It was simply different shades of grass. There were dozens of hearts, everywhere, all intertwined together..."

"They're united," another woman said.

We stood in silence, gazing out at the vast field, now decorated beautifully with "united" hearts. It was a heavenly masterpiece, for sure.

After a few moments, we carried on. We walked the Stations of the Cross and then went back to the prayer center for the rosary service. About forty or fifty people gathered into the prayer center to pray. The lights dimmed and the soft recitation of prayer was like an echo from Heaven. Then we went home.

A few days later I saw one of the women who had gone on this trip at the grocery store.

"Oh, Stace!" She said. "I have to show you my pictures from the Shrine!"

She walked over to my car and pulled out a large stack. She leafed through them and pulled out one in particular. It was the group photo we took at the Lake of Angels.

"Look what's behind us," she said. "And remember I took this picture with that throw-away camera, which didn't have a flash."

I couldn't believe my eyes. Floating behind our group was a smiling angel made of pure light. He had short, curly hair and a very young-looking face. There was no mistaking it. It was not an abstract image. It was a clear, obvious angel.

What made this photo even more miraculous, however, was the group conversation we had just before we took this picture. I told the group that there was one angel from each of the nine choirs of angels stationed around the lake.

"Wouldn't it be neat if we could see them," one of the women said. We all agreed it would be, and then we took the picture.

"Neat, indeed," I thought, now staring directly at an angel in the picture. It was absolutely magnificent!

This picture unveiled a whole new dimension of the journey. It unveiled the entire community of believers—the faithful here on earth, working in conjunction with the holy souls in Purgatory, and the saints and angels in Heaven.

Clearly, our journeys are like the green hearts that my friends and I saw on that vast field. As we travel through life, we cannot allow ourselves to be blinded by the harsh elements of the journey—the cold and the dreariness. Instead, we must be attentive to what, and who, surrounds us. "Wait...look..." as one woman said.

We must be attentive to the Hand of the Father, Who has drawn each of our journeys and intertwined them with the journeys of so many other tiring souls—some who are lagging behind, some who are lost, some who are walking step by step with us, and some who are ahead of us (beyond the brambles) climbing that final hill through the flames of Purgatory.

The good news, though, is that there are just as many souls to help us, as there are souls for us to help. We have the assistance of the saints, who have already traveled the way, suffered the flames, and conquered the maze. We have the angels, who from the beginning of time have guarded the path, guided its travelers, and brought light to what often lies hidden. And let's not forget those holy souls in

Purgatory. Though suffering as they are, they still pray for us—even if they can't pray for themselves.

Jesus illustrated this cooperative effort when He told Maureen, "My Mother...has taken this petition—the victory of Holy Love in hearts—to the holy souls in Purgatory. They are praying with you, along with the Church Triumphant in Heaven." (May 5, 2002)

Listen, my friends to these words; take heart in the message, and carry on with confidence. Know that you are not alone, not by far. For what an immense community you are a part of, what a vast and beautiful body is this mystical Body of Christ! Therefore, be joyful in the way. And thank God for the precious gift that is the Church.

CHAPTER 17

"The Shackles"

*"My brothers and sisters, My Divine Love and Divine Mercy
transcend time and space to come to you to offer you
entrance into the Chambers of Our United Hearts. As I have
so lovingly and mercifully offered these Chambers to you, so
you must go forward in the world and offer them to your
brothers and sisters around you. I will refuse no one, even the
hardest sinner, if they would turn to Me with remorse."*
~Jesus (September 6, 2002)

*"My Kingdom begins and ends in everyone today who allows
it. Let your faults and failings rise up in your hearts today and
slip away as a droplet of water evaporates in the atmosphere
of My Mercy.*
~Jesus (June 9, 1999)

*My mercy is without blemish and irreversible. My Mercy pours
upon an erring heart that turns to Me with sorrow." "Think of
Divine Mercy as a sweet spring breeze that blows refreshingly
across your face after a gentle rain. It invigorates you and
inspires you to pick yourself up and start anew. If you could
feel the touch of My Mercy, it would be as a gentle caress of
your soul, reassuring you and strengthening you for the road
ahead."*
~Jesus (September 11, 1999)

As Easter approached, I felt myself slipping backwards on the journey. I told you before that I am one of the weaker souls walking this path. I struggled for years with many serious health problems, but the ones that were most difficult were those related to food—erratic blood sugars, food allergies/sensitivities, and gluttony. They call it one of the seven deadly sins but it is especially fatal for me.

I have had to watch my diet very carefully—avoiding sugars and processed carbohydrates. Otherwise, I am a mess. I'm irritable, exhausted, and physically inept, to say the least. Excess sugar and carbs can set off this domino effect in my body, resulting in other health issues too. However, sugary foods and carbs are often what I crave the most.

Therefore, the few weeks before Easter were especially trying. There was no shortage of candy lying around. At first, I ate a bit of chocolate. Next, I ate just a part of a cinnamon roll (and I have a gluten allergy). Then I ate the rest of the cinnamon roll, frosting included. I continued with many more cinnamon rolls, which sent me on a rampage of gluttony, eating everything in sight.

Needless to say, I was not able to pray after that. In fact, I was not able to do much of anything. My heart was racing, I was light-headed, my body was heavy and swollen. My hormones and emotions were on a rollercoaster. I was impatient, crying, and altogether nasty. Not only did I quit focusing on my family, I quit cleaning the house, and I quit writing the book.

The worst part was that my _desires_ changed. I no longer _wanted_ to do these things. Depression, despair and hopelessness had entered the scene. _No one is going to read the book anyway,_ I thought. _I'm just a young, no-name author writing about some unapproved Shrine._

I had about given up. I continued sneaking sugary food, and my life was a drag, joyless and hard. I was bleak, impatient, critical, apathetic, and selfish. I was everything that I previously had tried so hard _not_ to become. I was in all ways contradictory to Holy Love.

I gave consent to the flesh, to gluttony. St. John of the Cross discussed this in his book _Ascent to Carmel._ "An unruly desire causes torment, fatigue, weariness, blindness and weakness."

He used Solomon as an example. "Who would have said that a man so perfect in wisdom and the gifts of God as Solomon would have been reduced to such blindness and foolishness of the will as to make altars to so many idols and to adore them himself, when he was old? And no more was needed to bring him to this than the affection which he had for his wives and his neglect to deny his desires... it is true that at the beginning he was cautious, nevertheless, because he denied them not, they gradually blinded and darkened his understanding, so that in the end, they succeeded in quenching that great light of wisdom which God had given him..."

I had done exactly this. It was an awful what gluttony had done to me... the state I was now in as a result of my weakness with food.

St. John of the Cross said the soul is to be like the Ark of the Covenant in Isaiah. "God commanded that the altar whereon the Ark of the Covenant was to be laid should be hollow within, so that the soul may understand how completely empty of all things God desires it to be, that it may be an altar worthy of the presence of His Majesty."

He said we should be "empty". But I was not. I abandoned the Lord for what? A few morsels of food? I threw out my fervor for a few seconds of hollow taste. I took hold of the devil's chains, his shackles, and I tied them around myself, just for a few minutes of pleasure. Oh how easy they go on... but how difficult they are to get off.

For this reason, I began saying a Divine Mercy novena—nine days of prayer for the Lord's Mercy—beginning on Good Friday and ending on Divine Mercy Sunday (the Sunday after Easter).

"Understand, My brothers and sisters," Jesus said, "if you have followed this most powerful novena to My Divine

Mercy, all guilt for past sin has been eliminated, as too, all punishment." (April7 2002)

I was scheduled to leave for Maranatha Spring at the end of the novena, so I hoped this prayer time would also help to prepare me for the much-needed pilgrimage. Jesus promised Maureen He would appear Saturday night, just after midnight, for Divine Mercy Sunday. What's more, Wayne Weible was to speak at the United Hearts Field the following afternoon. I was anxious to hear him since it was his book, *Medjugorje: The Message,* that Our Lady used to convince me to write the original apparitions article in *The Gist* magazine.

The day I was to leave for the shrine, however, the temptations returned. Surprisingly, they weren't temptations toward gluttony, but were nonetheless indirect temptations to abandon prayer. It was apathy combined with car trouble. This is in addition to the fact that my husband was out of town, my kids weren't feeling well, and the babysitter wasn't sure when she would be available.

I decided just to cancel the trip. *It's just not worth it,* I thought.

But as quickly as the thought came to me, I realized these inconveniences were an attack. I realized it was such a strong attack *not* to go, because there was a big reason why I *should* go. Somehow, I just knew I needed to be at Holy Love.

Through the grace of God, I persevered. I went to confession and repented of my numerous failures. I went to Mass. Then, I dropped the kids off at my mother-in-law's. And even though I spilled an entire blueberry pie (which was to be her thank you gift) all over my last clean pair of jeans, I got on the road and headed for Ohio (purple, sticky stains and all).

Once there, I went straight for the Prayer Center. I put a petition on the Blessing Point—a very personal, heartfelt note to the Blessed Mother:

"Immaculate Mary, Oh Blessed Mother,

*I do not know if I can, or if I **should** ask this of You—You Who have already shed so much grace on me, and have already blessed me so abundantly— but I beg You: plead for me to Your Son, that He might take this gluttony from me. I cannot overcome it myself. I have tried, but I am weak, so weak. Mother, I ask this of You for one reason: because this temptation I know, is a barrier between me and Your Son. And more than anything, I want to be closer to Him. I want to be united to Him. I know I am not worthy of this grace that I seek, but I ask for it anyway, because I am desperate for Him—He is my only Strength and means of Salvation. Please have mercy on me...I love You both dearly. Amen."*

I folded up my petition, placed it on the blessing point, kissed it and then placed it in the basket at Our Lady's feet. I took a deep breath in, and I felt hopeful again.

When I turned around, I saw Mary Ann. "Hi Stacy," she said. "I have a message for you." She told me that Don and Maureen wanted me to sit in the tent with them during the apparition.

"Oh... okay," I said, feeling a little apprehensive. I always thought the tent was just for the priests.

"Just see Jane when you get to the field and she'll direct you."

I nodded, then I went back out to my car. I got my rosary and put on a heavier coat, some gloves, a hat and a scarf. It was Divine Mercy Sunday but the snow was really coming down, and the temperature was dropping.

Even still, thousands showed up at the Field of the United Hearts to pray. Some were sitting in folding chairs, wrapped in blankets. Others knelt in the snow, venerating the statues of the United Hearts.

As I walked to the tent I watched the snowflakes. I began to marvel at how fitting the weather was for this particular feast day. As Jesus said on Divine Mercy Sunday in 2003, "Understand that today I make the most scarlet of sins as white as snow."

"Hi, Stacy!" Jane said. "Come on in. Maureen and Don usually sit over there," she said, pointing to the right side of the tent. "The rest of us sit wherever there is room." There were many long rows of chairs set up, and I took a seat at the far left side of the tent, trying to be as inconspicuous as possible. Many priests and a few nuns filed in after me and I felt out of place—VERY out of place.

I put my head down to pray and so I hadn't noticed that Maureen and Don had come in. Within minutes the service began. At the third Glorious Mystery—the Decent of the Holy Spirit—Jesus came.

"Please kneel." MaryAnn said, over the speaker system.

I dropped to my knees, as did thousands of others, in the cold wet, slushy snow. I kept my head down and prayed for Mercy. I was so caught up in the moment that I didn't look over at Maureen. Maybe I should have, at least for the sake of this book—so that I could describe for you what took place.

But honestly, in that moment, it wasn't about the book. I felt in my heart that I was in the presence of the Lord and there was nothing that could have pulled me out of a position of utmost reverence for my God. Besides, it was not Maureen's demeanor or facial expressions during the apparition that would have convinced me of its authenticity.

It was the power that settled in the air and the love that enveloped my heart that convicted me.

Minutes later the rosary resumed and many took their seats again. I kept my head down as I prayed, and then there was a tap on my shoulder.

"Maureen would like to see you." Mary Ann said.

But she's all the way over there, I thought to myself, a bit nervous about squeezing through the dozens of priests and nuns that were currently in prayer.

I got up from my seat and my legs were shaking. In fact, my whole body was shaking—like from the inside, but not from the cold, though. Something happened to me during that apparition, something very powerful. I made my way through the chairs. Fr. Mike stood up to give me his chair, and I took a seat next to Maureen. We finished the rosary and she leaned over to me.

"We gave the draft of the book to Wayne," she whispered. "He said that we got the right person for the job." She smiled and patted me on the back, as if to say 'well done'. She then quickly introduced me to Wayne, who I didn't realize, was sitting right next to her.

"This is Stacy," she said to him.

He smiled wide, took off his glove, and we shook hands. "Ohh," he said. "Hi!"

"It's very nice to meet you," I told Him.

A few minutes later they were gone and I was sitting in a tent full of priests waiting to hear a message from Jesus. It was all very surreal, I have to say.

Mary Ann began to read the message that had just been given. Jesus said, "I am your Jesus, born Incarnate. Once again I come to address all people and all nations. During these tenuous times, it is the Father's Will that the floodgate of My Mercy open upon all mankind...But I cannot, and will not force the sinner to approach Me. He must first, with a repentant heart, approach Me. How I desire to resolve all that distracts the soul from the path of My Provision. I cannot give to you what you refuse to receive...

"You do not realize the breadth and depth of the abyss between Heaven and earth. The abyss I describe to you represents mankind's relationship with the Eternal Father; thus the Divine Will...The choices that man makes with his free will either separates or unites him to Me...The greatest outpouring of My Mercy awaits the greatest sinner. All that stands between any sinner and My Divine Mercy is the soul's free will. With an anguished Heart I await his repentance...

"If the heart of the world—the soul of all humanity— would grasp this truth, you would see an end to moral degeneration, terrorism, wars, both in hearts and in the world, disease and famine, both spiritual and physical. Realize this truth, My dear brothers and sisters. I come to you in sincerity, seeking your welfare and salvation...

"Tonight, My brothers and sisters, you experience the cold. I experience always the coldness of hearts in the world; but you will not have a cold heart if you accept My Mercy...Tonight I am taking many temptations far from certain hearts. I am endorsing certain projects, and through God's Eternal Will many hearts will be changed." (April 14, 2007)

As I sat there, I replayed the message in my mind. "He's taking certain temptations far from certain hearts?" I wondered about my earlier petition to the Blessed Mother. "And endorsing certain projects?" I recalled my earlier concern that I was just a no-name author in need of some "bigger name" to endorse my work.

I smiled, thinking, *If Jesus is endorsing this book, then I guess I have nothing to worry about. With God, all things are possible.*

As translators read the message in Spanish and then Korean, I made my way back to the car, and drove to a nearby motel for the night. In the morning I went to Mass and then back over to the Shrine for Wayne's talk. Surprisingly, the sun came out. The snow from the night before had completely melted and it was almost warm—in spite of the forecast which predicted more snow.

At this point, thousands of people were already at the Field. I noticed many of them were pointing up at the sky. I turned my head upward to see what they were looking at, but it was too bright.

"Shield your eyes," one woman told me, holding her hand to her forehead like a visor. I imitated her and again looked up.

"Oh my..." I gasped.

It was as if I was staring at an eclipse of light. There was something like a large, flat host—though bright and dazzling—in the sky directly in front of the sun. And it was pulsating. It was beating, like a human heart. Rays were streaming out from behind the host in various colors and they were spinning quickly like the hand on a stop watch.

As I watched it pulsate, the sky behind it changed. What normally appeared like a flat, blue blanket became dark pink, and took on other dimensions. The sky revealed such depth! It was as if it formed a vacuum, or a path...and you could see into the Heavens. Immediately, I thought of the message from the night before, "You do not realize the breadth and depth of the abyss between Heaven and earth," Jesus said.

We stood there for several minutes, and I recalled Jesus' words to St. Faustina, "My Heart overflows with great mercy for souls, especially for poor sinners...For them, I dwell in the tabernacle as King of Mercy"[15] I couldn't help but marvel at what a beautiful gift this was for Divine Mercy Sunday: a glowing, pulsating host—representing Sacrament of Mercy—which seemed on this day, to have vanquished the cold.

This too, was just as Jesus said the night before, "Tonight...you experience the cold...but you will not have a cold heart if you accept My Mercy."

The sun returned to its normal state after a few minutes. Then, Wayne began speaking, and I was deeply touched by everything he said. I felt such a familiarity with his story...his fervor for the Lord and Our Lady, his insecurities, mistakes and undeserved calling.

At 3:00 P.M., after Wayne finished speaking, we said the Chaplet of Divine Mercy, a United Hearts Chaplet, and the Glorious mysteries of the Rosary. During the Rosary Jesus appeared to Maureen.

"Today My Mercy rests upon you," Jesus said, "helping you to understand how you can best serve Me. Once again, I am placing the seal of My Blessing upon certain and profound endeavors that have come to light in the last few days, some in the last few hours. Those whom are inspired will recognize My call."

---

[15] Diary: Divine Mercy in My Soul, Marian Press; 3rd edition, February 2005 pg. 367

"Today the Hearts of Jesus and Mary are greatly appeased by your loving presence here amidst great adversity. I'm writing on your hearts the Messages of the Chambers of the United Hearts. You will not forget them. You will propagate them with much energy. My brothers and sisters: spread these Messages according to the Divine Will of My Eternal Father." (April 15, 2007)

When we finished praying, Mary Ann thanked everyone for coming. Then she said, "Stacy M. if you're in the audience, please call Don Kyle's cell phone."

Stacy M? Uh oh. I think that's me. I thought. *Rats. I didn't bring my cell phone.* Too embarrassed to ask someone to borrow theirs, I walked over to the tent and found Fr. Mike.

"Don and Maureen want to know if you can come back to the house with us and Wayne," he said.

"Sure," I agreed.

"That is, as soon as he's done..." Father smiled, nodding towards him. There was a line of people waiting to meet Wayne, and he was patiently and cordially speaking with each one of them. I didn't mind waiting for him in the least. In fact, watching him—the way he kindly ministered to each one of them. It was a very moving experience for me.

Eventually, he did finish though, and we walked back to see Don and Maureen.

"It's just going to be you and Wayne," Don said to me, smiling and handing me the draft I had written. "Maureen and I have a meeting."

Never in a million years could I have imagined what would come next.

"I've read the draft of what you have so far," Wayne said. "It's good, real good. And I'd like to help you with it. If it's okay with you, I'd like to write the Foreword for it."

I just sat there. I couldn't believe my ears. I was speechless.

"I'll be honest with you," he said. "I get so many manuscripts sent to me, so many people asking me to edit things and do forewords...and I always send them back, because I just don't have the time...But I don't know...This is different."

I knew exactly what was different. As Jesus had said just moments earlier, "I am placing the seal of My Blessing upon certain and profound endeavors...Those whom are inspired will recognize My call..."

It seemed to me, Wayne was one of those who were inspired. It also seemed it was by way of this best-selling author, Wayne Weible, that Jesus was choosing to endorse this book. And I can't tell you how grateful this no-name was.

Wayne and I talked for awhile about the book, and then we talked about the journey. We talked about our families, Our Lady and the Church. He was so kind with his words and so generous with his time, that I could barely find words to thank him. He gave me his contact information and after a few more minutes I left.

I walked outside and headed toward the Prayer Center. I looked at my watch. It was 4:30 P.M. I realized that I had eaten only half of a spinach omelet in over 30 hours, a miracle for me, as I normally must eat every three hours or so to keep my blood sugars on an even keel.

Surprisingly, though, I felt fine. I felt better than fine. In fact, I felt like the shackles were off! I wasn't totally healed of all my health problems that day, but I was freed for a time. ** I cannot accurately tell you what was swirling about in my heart as I walked back to the prayer center. I realized how small I was, how undeserving I was, and yet at the same time, how very loved and cherished I was in the eyes of God.

Once at the Prayer Center, I went over to the alcove. I wanted just to drop to my knees and thank the Blessed Mother for answering my petition, but there were people already kneeling there. So I gave them their space and stood behind them and began to silently pray—not with words, though. It was more of a feeling, or an intensity, that just lifted directly from my heart.

I then noticed a song playing softly in the background. It was the hymn *Here I Am Lord*, based on the story of Isaiah's commissioning, recorded in Isaiah 6. In this story, Isaiah saw the Lord in vision (6:1-4). Immediately, he confessed his sinful and unworthy state, "Woe is me!" he said, "For I am undone; because I am a man of unclean lips, and I dwell in the midst of a people of unclean lips." (5:5).

But the Lord had mercy on him. An angel took a burning coal from God's Altar, touched it to Isaiah's lips, and said, "Lo, this hath touched thy lips; and thy iniquity is taken away, and thy sin forgiven." (6:7).

The Lord then asked, "Whom shall I send...who will go for us?" (6:8)

Isaiah replied "Here I am; send me." Being filled with such gratitude for God's Mercy, he took on his ministry as a prophet. He agreed to work for the Lord, so that all might know the love and mercy he himself had just received. (6:8-10).

And God told him, "Go, and tell this people." (6:9)

I stood in front of Our Lady's alcove, listening to that song, recalling that Scripture...and oh, if only I could describe for you exactly what happened to me there in that moment. If only language contained the words to explain the effect our Lord's Mercy had on my poor soul.

I always thought mercy was as if to say, *I see what you have done to me but I will forgive you anyway.* But I came to see that the Lord's Mercy is something entirely different.

The Lord's Mercy is as if to say, *I am so blinded by love for you that I no longer see what you have done to Me.*

"I do not remember your last profanity against Holy Love," Jesus said. "Once you commit your transgressions to My Mercy, all is forgiven and forgotten." (August 2, 1999)

Even still, His Mercy does more than wipe us clean and bring us current in our debt. Because He is not *average* in generosity or charity, His Mercy pours into our lives most abundantly, creating a *surplus* of grace, an *excess* of blessing.

"I am ready to give you **more** than your deepest desires..." He said. (April 22, 2001 Divine Mercy Sunday) And truly, He did that for me.

I did not deserve to be forgiven of my gluttony and the many sins that resulted from it. The way that I had succumbed to temptations and acted without love, it was appalling, really. But thankfully, His Love for me was greater and more unconditional than my love for Him.

His Mercy changed me entirely. It was just like He said, "...there is more to My Divine Mercy than forgiveness. My Mercy comes to you as the grace which convicts your conscience and...brings together the human soul and the Divine Will of My Father." (Oct 16, 2004)

For the first time in my life I didn't think about what the Will of the Father was, or what trials it would bring. I thought only of how much I loved it, how undeserving I was

295

to participate in it, and how much I wanted the fulfillment of it—regardless of what it would cost me.

Finally, I understood what Jesus meant when He said, "My Divine Mercy and My Divine Love unite to form My Victory," (July 4, 2001) It's the very Mercy of God—the fruit of His Love for us—which transforms the human heart and gently propels it toward sanctity and unity!

What's more, as I pondered the entire day, the song *Here I Am*, and the Scripture, I came to see that the Virgin Mary was like the angel in Isaiah 6...and the burning coal that She took from the Altar of God was none other than the Flame of Divine Love and Divine Mercy—the very Sacred Heart of Jesus, pierced as a perfect Sacrifice to reconcile us with God.

"...just as Holy Love prepares the heart for Divine Love," Jesus explained, "Holy Mercy prepares the heart for Divine Mercy." (February 6, 2004)

Truly, it was Mary who heard my cry at that Blessing Point, and it was through Her Heart—the purest channel of Holy Mercy—that Divine Mercy came and touched my unclean lips. And like Isaiah, it was then that I understood my mission.

It was just like Jesus said a few hours earlier, "Today My Mercy rests upon you, helping you to understand how you can best serve Me." (April 15, 2007)

296

Standing there in front of the Blessed Mother's alcove—in front of the same statue where my mom had encountered the Divine Mercy Jesus—I too experienced Mercy. I felt such a consuming gratitude that it incited me to hand over to God every ounce of my life—the life He had just restored. And I vowed, with all my heart, to live the Consecration. I agreed to be all His through Her, to be an instrument of love and mercy in their battle, to give to other souls all that Jesus and Mary had just given to me.

And now, here I am, back to writing this book—not because I somehow merited it but because God in His great mercy stood me back up on the path, and through the Sacrament of Reconciliation, breathed sanctifying grace into a glutton. He picked off a deadened leaf and a new bud of possibility bloomed.

The shackles have lost their power in the presence of Mercy. Truly now I can say with the Lord, "My food is to do the will of the one who sent me and complete His work." (John 4:34)

Now, here I am, dancing in the rays of the Son once again. Here I am, full of life.

Standing in the alcove, the song played, "Whom shall I send?"

And I cried, "Here I am, Lord."

*** The Lord continued to lead me to healing after that day. It was not an instant healing, but rather a step by step healing that He provided through education. I began to learn about what was happening in my body. I began to learn how certain foods and various supplements could help. This feeling of renewal and gratitude prompted me to pursue a health coach certification so that I could help others as well. Today my health-coaching business is called "Rebuilding Your Temple" (www.RebuildingYourTemple.com) and is part of a wholistic approach to wellness: mind, body and SOUL.*

CHAPTER 19

"The End"

"My brothers and sisters, I come to you today with My needs, and I am hopeful that you will listen attentively and act on My needs. Do not wait for the next present moment, but act in this present moment to achieve what I require. The way to world peace is only through Holy and Divine Love. Therefore, I am seeking this worldwide consecration to Our United Hearts so that the heart of the world can be affected towards the change for good. This way the grace will be given to all political leaders to see their errors and their sins against love. I am counting on My church leaders—all church leaders, all ecclesiastics—to carry out My requests."

~Jesus (September 15, 2007)

"As your Mother, I come with a love beyond all telling to lead you, protect you and show you the way. This is the most I can do. I cannot make you choose Holy Love. I cannot make you respect God and neighbor. You, dear children, must decide to come closer to God. You must desire to pray and to sacrifice for those who do not make good choices. You must decide for Holy Love. Do not be surprised as I tell you that this site of Heaven's predilection will come into focus in the near future. Heaven desires greater, more positive attention be drawn to these messages. While Satan has held sway with his lies and innuendos, Heaven will now intervene. Truth will win out."

~Blessed Mother (June 4, 2005)

"I come to you, as I always do, to change the heart of the world through Holy and Divine Love. This, indeed, is My sole purpose for being in your midst. It is the reason Heaven communicates with earth at this site. It is the cause of all the miracles and graces here at this site of predilection—to change the thoughts, words and actions of all humanity into Holy Love."

~Jesus (October 5, 2005)

Well, we have come to the final chapter of this book. And I must admit: I have written this chapter several times—each time with dissatisfaction. Thus far, I just have not been able to "see" the end of this story. I have not been able to visualize where this is going.

But I am not the first to have trouble understanding. At that last supper, just before His death, Jesus told his apostles, "You know where I am going..."

Thomas, however, said, "No, we don't know, Lord. We haven't any idea where you are going..." (John 14:4-5)

The apostles walked with Jesus for three years. They listened to His teachings, His promises for salvation, His predictions concerning His passion and death...and yet, they still could not "see" how the story would end.

Oh, how I feel their pain.

For over a decade, I have been traveling back and forth to Ohio, doing interviews, reading and studying the messages given to Maureen, comparing them with approved texts. And yet, I was still like those first disciples, crying, "Lord, I haven't any idea where this is going!"

It was almost unbelievable that I didn't know. At the very beginning of this story Jesus actually told Maureen what He wanted the title of this book to be. She handed me a piece of paper in one of our interviews that read, "A Pilgrim's Journey Into the Divine Will."

By giving her the title, He summarized for me what He wanted the book to be about—a step by step account of a soul trying to live in God's Will, which is nothing more than Holy Love in the present moment. And yet, knowing this, I still couldn't see the end. I had the title, the map, the grace, and the mercy to complete this project. It was all tucked down deep in the back pack of my heart. And yet, arriving at the finish, I felt as lost as I was at the beginning.

I was truly a pilgrim—like an Israelite—journeying through an unfamiliar land. Because of this, it took me more than 11 years to finalize this book. Eleven years! It's humbling, really.... actually, it's embarrassing. I've been so close to the end, and yet (without knowing how to proceed), so very far away. But maybe, just maybe, that's the whole point...

My friends, we are very blessed to be part of this generation, because we know what the apostles did not know when they walked with the Lord—we know the end of this story! We know that, in the end, Victory belongs to Jesus. Because of the messages given to Maureen, we now even know _how_ this Victory will come about.

It will come about one heart at a time, as each one is united to God in Holy Love. My friends, eleven years ago I was sitting in my office watching a Windows XP logo dance across my computer monitor, wondering how to proceed with my writing. (You might remember it from chapter one.) It was much like now, actually. Then, I picked up a book by Wayne Weible and Our Lady spoke to my heart, inviting me into this journey. I took a small, seemingly insignificant, step and went investigating apparitions in Ohio.

At that site I was shown the map, the entryway, the path, the destination, the chambers, the hurdles and the strategy. I joined a vehicle of prayer. I discovered the Light of God in the Eucharist and experienced a transformation. I met resistance and failed many times, but I experienced renewal in His Mercy.

Who could have imagined what chasing the messages of the Virgin Mary would do to my life? Who could have envisioned what a small "yes" could have unleashed in my soul? Never could I have dreamed that I would be finishing this book, or that Wayne Weible would have written the Foreword for it.

But this is how it has happened—as you should know. You have been with me in these pages, throughout my journey. And it is not an accident that we have spent this time together. Rather, it has been by the grace of God, given to both of us through the Immaculate Heart of the Virgin Mary. It is no more accidental that you are reading my testimony now, than it was accidental I had read Wayne's testimony back then.

In fact, pause here for just a minute. Please. Quiet yourself in your soul. And listen... This, friend, is _your_ invitation...

I have been sitting here for so long, knowing full-well the story of Holy and Divine Love...yet unsure how to proceed, unsure how to write this last chapter, which I know is to be a summation of all that has been unveiled. But now, I think I finally have come to my conclusion. It is this: I simply _cannot_ write the end of this story... not without you, that is.

You see, through these pages, the Virgin Mary is calling _you_ onto the path. The Mother of God is summoning _you_ to the journey—a journey where each new footstep writes a new testimony and each new testimony invites a new heart.

Therefore, each of you, my friends, has a responsibility in writing this last chapter. Each of you has a unique role to play in this unfolding Victory of the United Hearts! For the Author of Life has written each of us into this script...but thus far, we have been slow in responding to the call. Much like my fingers on this keyboard, we have been slow in moving forward to our end.

Why? My guess is because these messages from Heaven strike a nerve in nearly every heart that hears them—after all, "all of us have strayed away like sheep. We have left God's paths to follow our own." (Is. 53:6) Even some shepherds have been led astray, as we've seen. But we must move forward.

Over the years, this is exactly what Holy Love Ministries has done—move forward. In spite of the resistance from the Diocese, they continue to advance. The Lord and our Blessed Mother continue to lead them and guide them, and the ministry continues to grow and flourish. Clearly it has the hand of God upon it.

The property now has a new prayer center that is much larger than the small red building that I first visited eleven years ago. There are many other new buildings too, even a chapel, as well as solar panels and wind mills. Mary, the Protectress of the Faith has been protecting this mission that courageously propagates the true faith. And I firmly believe that someday this _will_ be a Church approved apparition site. But probably not for awhile. So, what do we do in the meantime?

We trust the Father's plan. We consecrate ourselves, right now, to the United Hearts and take a step forward onto the path of Holy Love. This revelation—these messages—are scripturally sound and are not contrary to any Church teaching. The Diocese did _not_ condemn them. They did not forbid people from going there or from reading the messages.

So, my friends, you have nothing to fear, but everything to gain. Begin now, to love God above all else and your neighbor as yourself in every present moment and see for yourself the good fruit it can produce. (If you need assistance, I have written a do-it-yourself retreat called _Victory in the Spiritual Garden._ This is a short, nine-chapter book that can be done as a novena. It takes you deeper into the journey, along the path of Holy Love, through the chambers. You can look for it on Amazon.com.)

Then, once you begin to live this journey, others will take notice—family, friends, co-workers. Soon even leaders of churches and nations will hear their call...which Jesus said is simply this:

"I request all church leaders, prelates—yes, the Holy Father himself—join together in consecrating the heart of the world to the United Hearts of Jesus and Mary," (September 15, 2007)

The Eternal Father added, "When you hear My Voice through this Message, accomplish My request...I speak to all churches, all governments, all ecclesiastics. If enough accomplish this and answer My request, you will gradually see governments change their policies, and finally, the heart of the world will return to innocence." (September 18, 2007)

Understand, my friends, that one consecrated heart leads to one consecrated household and family. One consecrated family leads to a consecrated community, then a nation. And one consecrated nation leads to a consecrated world! The messages of Holy and Divine Love contained in this book are meant for all people of all nations! This is the Triumph we've been waiting for! This is the Victory. This is how it will all come to an end. This is the remedy for all of the woes of the world.

That being said, we have reached a very decisive point in this story. All has been unveiled now. This is the last act, and the Blessed Mother has come to earth with a curtain call for souls—a call She told Maureen, is "Heaven's _Last_ Call to Humanity" (September 24, 1998).

Of all the apparitions that the Blessed Mother has given over the centuries in every corner of the world— Fatima, Lourdes, Knock, everywhere—She says this revelation of Holy Love is the last. Why? Perhaps, because many believe we have entered the last battle of good versus evil. Sr. Lucia of Fatima once said, "The Final confrontation between the Lord and Satan will be over marriage and the family...this is the decisive issue."

It is not hard to see that we have arrived at that point—the 100th anniversary of Fatima—a time when coincidentally marriage is no longer between a man and a woman and parents can legally kill their children through abortion. Did the visionary of Fatima predict this time period?

We don't know for certain. But we do know there is a battle taking place in every present moment on the battlefield of the human heart. The battle to choose or not choose Holy Love, the battle to choose God above else or self above all else. This is the decisive choice. Will we choose God and His laws, first in every instance? Will we choose to love our neighbor as ourselves?

The Eternal Father told Maureen, "Priorities must be reestablished so that self and the world no longer reign over free will. Pleasing Me—loving Me—should be the impetus behind your free-will choices. It is then all things will come to completion according to My Divine Will." (August 20, 2017)

God is watching this battle carefully; the Saints are praying earnestly; and the angels are taking their places promptly. All are in anticipation for the inevitable Victory of

God's holy children and the reign of Jesus Christ on earth. All that remains now is how many of us will choose it. Christ has won the Victory, but will you be part of it?

We cannot remain indifferent to this call, to this invitation. We cannot stand neutral in the center of this battlefield, declaring "This war does not concern me". For I tell you: if you are breathing, then this war concerns you. As long as you have life within you, the prince of death seeks the ruin of your soul. Do not be unaware of this truth. Do not be caught off guard in the hunt, lest you be swept away and taken as a prisoner in this war.

"Satan has edged his way into every segment of society," Jesus said. "He is influencing medicine, technology, entertainment, the news media, governments, literature and political issues. His influence is so insidious the general population does not notice his grasp... He is pulling souls away from Me at an ever-increasing rate." (October 24, 2007)

Therefore, we must choose. No, it will not be easy. Not everyone will understand why you have chosen this life, this path. But time is running out. This is Heaven's last call. We have come to the final chapter of this story, and while the end is decided, it is still unwritten. The remaining pages are still blank.

So I beg you: help me write them. Let this not have a sad ending for our already-Sorrowful Mother and Her Son, the Eternal Victim. Instead, let us put our heads together—no, let us put our hearts together—and step forward onto the path. You now are the pilgrim, friend, and this now is your journey.

This is only in this way that the story of Holy and Divine Love can ever come to completion. So, please, make the decision now, in this present moment, and join me for a walk. Help me write a magnificent story of triumph and glory for God, Our Father. And someday we will arrive at the victor's tent together. We will cross the threshold of eternity, gloriously uttering the words of our dying Savior, "It is finished."

Made in the USA
Lexington, KY
23 August 2017